The Books of The Maccabees includes new translations of the first, second, third, and forth books of The Maccabees. The Books of The Maccabees uses the Aramaic and Greek with the previous versions compared and revised. The Translator hopes that acknowledging the Jewish origins of these books can help us better understand their contents.

Also From Dr JS Trimm:

The Middle Pillar – A Jewish Perspective on the Godhead

Seven Seals Seven Thunders

Hebraic Roots Version Complete Bible

Sefer Chanoch – The Book of Enoch

HEBRAIC-ROOTS COMMENTARY ON THE "NEW TESTAMENT" IN THIRTEEN VOLUMES
1. Matthew
2. Mark
3. Luke
4. Yochanan
5. Acts
6. The Jewish Epistles: Ya'akov, 1 & 2 Kefa, 1 ,2,& 3 Yochanan, Y'hudah
7. Romans
8. 1&2Corinthians
9. Galatians, Ephesians, Philippians, Colosians
10. 1&2 Thessalonians
11. 1&2 Timothy, Titus & Philemon
12. Hebrews
13.Revelation

And soon to be realeased:

Interlinear Hebrew 'Book of Enoch

Interlinear Hebrew 'Book of Jasher

Interlinear Hebrew 'Book of Mathew

Interlinear Hebrew 'Book of Hebrews

Aramaic Gospels Project

Aramaic Emmissaries Project

ARAMAIC REVELATION PROJECT

THE BOOKS OF THE MACCABEES

1ST 2ND 3RD & 4TH MACCABEES

The
Books
of the
Maccabees
A Messianic Channukah Edition

1st 2nd 3rd and 4th Maccabees

Translated out of the Aramaic and Greek
with the previous versions
compared and revised.

By
James Scott Trimm

Had Pasot Beit David
Beaverton, Oregon
http://www.hadpasot-beitdavid.com

Published on behalf of
Institute for Nazarene Jewish Studies

First Edition, Second Printing
8th Month 5766 (May 2006)
Printed in USA

Had Pasot Beit David (House of David Printing Co)
PO Box ###
Beaverton OR 97008-6052
(503) 644-4149
www.hadpasot-beitdavid.com

Institute for Nazarene Jewish Studies
Box 471
Hurst, TX 76053
(817) 284-7039
http://www.nazarene.net
sanj@nazarene.net

Cover design and concept by Penguin Design, Beaverton, Oregon, USA.
Printed in USA on demand by Lulu Press

Table of Contents

INTRODUCTION

What is Channukah?

Channukah is a celebration of the victory of Judaism over Greek culture. When Alexander conquered much of the known world, it was his dream to bring the Greek culture to the world. Upon his death his Empire was divided among his generals. Each of these new Kingdoms were Greek in culture. In time the Syrian "Seleucid Empire" came to be ruled by Antiochus Epiphanies who also gained control of Jerusalem. This coincided with a campaign of forced helization in Judea. Circumcision and Torah observance became outlawed. Jews were forced, on pain of death, to sacrifice unkosher animals on the alter, to rededicate the Temple to the Greek god Zeus and to eat meat that had been offered up to idols. In reaction to this oppression a group of Jewish warriors known as the Maccabees fled into the wilderness and fought gorilla warfare against the Greco-Syrians. They ultimately prevailed and rededicated the Temple to YHWH on the 25th of Kislev, establishing the eight day festival of Channukah to celebrate the rededication of the alter.

Channukah vs. Christmas

Often Channukah is confused with Christmas. Some have even said that Channukah is "Jewish Christmas" or "what the Jews call Christmas". This is most unfortunate. Christmas resulted when the Christian Church chose to incorporate pagan customs into their religion. Christmas was adopted from the very Hellenist culture that the Maccabees were resisting. Christmas is a capitulation to Hellenism while the point of Channukah is a celebration of the successful refusal to capitulate to Hellenism.

Long before Christmas, Channukah was celebrated as a "festival of lights". We learn from 2Maccabees (1:18 & 10:6) that Channukah was celebrated in the same manner as Sukkot (Tabernacles). And according to the Talmud Sukkot was celebrated by lighting up Jerusalem with four menorahs which stood 75 feet tall (m.Sukkah 5:2-4; b.Sukkah 52b). And while some believe that gift giving originated in Christmas and was adopted into Channukah, it was very likely the other way around, as Jewish fesivals were celebrated with gift giving at least as early as the time of Ester (Ester 9:22).

Channnukah and Torah

Channukah is very much a pro-Torah festival. The primary symbol of Channukah is light and light represents the Torah, as the Tanak says:

> For the commandment is a lamp;
> and the Torah is light...
> (Prov. 6:23)

The antagonists in the Books of the Maccabees are called in the Greek versions of these books "Torah-less" (anomian) and "Opposed to Torah" (para-nomian). The books of 2nd and 4th Maccabees tell us of those who were martyred because they refused to abandon Torah and the theme of the 4th Book of Maccabees is that the Torah (being divine reason) is supreme.

Channnukah and the Last Days

The festival of Channukah is a picture of the last days. As demonstrated in the following chart:

Last Days Events	Maccabean Events
The Apostasy (2Thes. 2:3)	Paganization of Israel (1Macc. 1:11-15)
The other "Jesus" (2Cor. 11:3-4; Mt. 7:20-23); the false prophet who causes people to follow the beast (Rev. 13:11-18; 19:20)	The preisthood is purchased by a certain "Yeshua" who prefers to go by his Greek name "Jason" and who leads the people to adopt pagan customs. (2Macc. 4:1-22)
The beast of Rev. 13 which is a composite of the four beasts of Dan. 7, commits the abomination of desolation refered to by Daniel. (Mt. 24:15; 2Thes. 2:1-4)	The desecration of the Temple by Antiochus Epiphanies. (1Macc. 1:41-64 & 2Macc. 6:1-6).
Tribulation (Mt. 24:9-13, 29)	Martyrs (2Macc. 6:7-31; 7; 4Macc. 5-18)

3 ½ years in which Y'hudah spends having fled into the wilderness. (Luke 21:20-24 & Rev. 12)	Judas (Y'hudah) and his family and allies to retreat into the Judean wilderness for three years.
Messiah who is both a Cohen (Priest) and a King prevails.	Y'hudah who becomes both a Cohen (Priest) and a King ultimately prevails.
A new Temple is dedicated (Ezek. 40-48) Tabernacles is celebrated by the world in the Kingdom. (Zech. 14:16-19)	The Temple is rededicated to YHWH with a belated celebration of Sukkot. (1Macc. 4:36-61; 2Macc. 10:1-9)
Only a small sealed remnant are found at Messiah's return (Rev. 12:17; Rev. 8). The Ark reveals its position (2Macc. 2:4-8)	Only one bottle of oil sealed by the High Priest is found hidden in the Temple (b.Shabbat 21b).

The Apocryphal Books of the Maccabees

The Books of the Maccabees are part of those books known as "Apocrypha". These are books which were not canonized in Rabbinic Judaism and were not preserved in the Hebrew of the Masoretic Text. They appear in the Greek Septuagint (in an appendix) and in the Peshitta Tanak (in an appendix) and also appear in the Latin Vulgate. Hebrew manuscripts of parts of some of the books of Apocrypha have turned up in the Cairo Geniza and among the Dead Sea Scrolls (but not any portion of the Books of the Maccabees).

All four books of the Maccabees appear in the appendices to the Septuagint and the Peshitta but the Latin Vulgate includes only 1st and 2nd Maccbees. In 1546 the Council of Trent decreed that the Roman Catholic Canon of the Old Testament includes most of the books of the Apocrypha including 1st and 2nd (but not 3rd and 4th) Maccabees. Most Protestant denominations maintain that the books of the Apocrypha (including those of the Maccabees) are useful for historic insight but should not be used as the basis for any doctrine.

Most scholars maintain that 1Maccabees was originally written in Hebrew, but that 2nd, 3rd and 4th Maccabees were originally written in Greek.

Origen tells us that the books of the Maccabees are called Σαρβηθ Σαρβαναι Ελ "Sarbeth sarbane el" which is clearly Hebrew. Scholars have debated what the underlying Hebrew is. The most obvious Hebrew would be: שר בית שר בני אל "Prince of the House of the Prince of the Sons of El." Torrey took Origin's transliteration to be a corruption of ספר בית השמנאי "Book of the House of the Hasmoneans".

The Four Levels and the Four Books of the Maccabees

In Jewish scriptural understanding it is maintained that a passage may be understood on any of four levels of understanding.

The first level of understanding is called PASHAT. Pashat means "simple" is the literal, simple meaning of the text.

The second level of understanding is called REMEZ. Remez means "hint" is the implied meaning of a passage"

The third level of understanding is called DRASH. Drash means "search" and is the homiletical or allegorical meaning of the text.

The fourth level of understanding is called SOD. Sod means "mystery" and is the hidden, secret or mystical meaning of the text.

The first letter from each of these words spells in Hebrew PaRDeS meaning "paradise".

The four Gospels are each written on each of the four levels of understanding of the life and teaching of Yeshua.

Mark gives the PASHAT, a short, simple, basic account of Yeshua's life with few details.

Luke gives the REMEZ and digs into the details and covers matters only hinted at in Mark.

Matthew gives the DRASH and presents the story as a narrative given as a narrative understanding of several cited passages from the Tanak.

Yochanan gives the SOD level understanding ad presents Messiah as the incarnate "Word".

In the same way the four books of the Maccabees are each written on each of these four levels.

1Maccabees gives the PASHAT, a short, simple account of the exploits of the Maccabees.

2Maccabees gives the REMEZ, digging into the details of the story not explored by 1Maccabees. The fifteen chapters of 2Maccabees cover the same material as the first seven chapters of 1Maccabees, but with much more information.

3Maccabees gives the DRASH level. 3Maccabees does not actually discuss the oppressions at the time of the Maccabees at all, but instead gives a related story of another oppression which took place some 50 years earlier, but which illustrates the same points as 1 & 2 Maccabees.

4Maccabees gives the SOD level. 4Maccabees uses the story of the Maccabees to demonstrate the supremacy of Torah as "divine reason" and as the "logos" (the "word" or "reason").

Some Notable Points in the Books of the Maccabees

The miracle of the oil

The miracle of the oil is not actually mentioned in the books of the Maccabees however the Talmud does recount it:

> What is the reason for Channukah? For our Rabbis taught: On the 25th of Kislev begin the days of Channukah, which are eight, during which lamentation for the dead and fasting are forbidden. For when the Greeks entered the Temple, they defiled all the oils in it, and when the Hasmonean dynasty prevailed against and defeated them, they [the Maccabees]

searched and found only one cruse of oil which possessed the seal of the High Priest, but which contained sufficient oil for only one day's lighting; yet a miracle occurred there and they lit [the lamp] for eight days. The following year these days were appointed a Festival with the recitation of Hallel and thanksgiving.
(b.Shabbat 21b)

While none of the books of the Maccabees mention this miracle, there are hints of it found in 2Maccabees (which is written on the REMEZ level). While the miracle of the oil is not included in the pashat of 2Maccabees, it is hinted at in the account of the preserved fire of the alter restored to the Temple rebuilt by Ezra and Nehemiah (2Macc. 1:19-36) and the account of the preservation of the tent, the ark and the alter of incense for the last days (2Macc. 2:4-8)

Moreover the miracle of the oil fits in very well with the last days imagery of the Channukah story. The remnant of the oil sealed by the High Priest represents the remnant believers who are sealed by the Ruach HaKodesh (Rev. 12:17; Rev. 8; Eph. 1:13). The Ruach HaKodesh is often symbolized in the Scriptures by the oil of the menorah (as in Zech. 4).

Things offered to idols

Several times the New Testament mentions the issue of "things offered to idols. In Acts 15:20, 29; 21:25 abstaining from "things offered to idols" is listed as one of the minimum levels of Torah observance Gentiles who are attending synagogue each week and hearing the Torah taught each week, must keep even before becoming circumcised as proselyte Jews. In Rev. 2:14, 20 eating "things offered to idols" is listed among the shortcomings of the assemblies in Pergamos and Thyatira.

In 1Cor. 8:1-13; 10:7, 14-19 Paul addresses the issue of eating "things offered to idols" as well. Now in these passages Paul agrees that one may not knowingly eat meat offered up to idols. The halachic issue Paul questions, is whether or not one must ask, when purchasing meat, whether or not it has been offered to idols. Paul argues (based on Ps. 24:1=1Cor. 10:26, 28) that meat is not actually altered by the idol but that eating such meat appears to others to endorse the idol to which it was offered. If meat is advertised as having been offered to idols, then believers may not eat it, since this would appear to endorse the idol. However, since the idol has no real power over the meat, believers are not required to ask, since this would imply that the believer believed that the idol had power over the meat, thus ascribing power to the idol and endorsing idolatry by acknowledging the idol's alleged power.

A basis for Paul's argument can be found by comparing Paul's summation of his argument in 1Cor. 10:28 to the story of the martyr Eleazar in 2Maccabbes 6:18-31 and 4Macc. 5-7. A major clue is given by the fact that the Greek New Testament uses the word ειδωλοθυτος for "things offered up to idols". This is exactly the same Greek word that is used in the Greek text of 4Maccabees 5:1-2:

> 1 The tyrant Antiochus, therefore, sitting in public state with his assessors upon a certain lofty place, with his armed troops standing in a circle around him,
> 2 commanded his spearbearers to seize every one of the Hebrews, and to compel them to taste swine's flesh, and things offered to idols[1].
> 3 And should any of them be unwilling to eat the accursed food, they were to be tortured on the wheel, and so killed.

Eleazer was a prominent Jew under the Helene rule. Eleazar was not willing to eat meat offered to idols, but because of his prominence, the authorities offered to allow him to sneak kosher meat into the feast and eat it instead, thus only appearing to eat meat offered up to idols. Eleazer refused, knowing that this would appear to endorse idolatry, despite the fact that the meat would be kosher. As a result Eleazar was executed. This story demonstrates that eating meat offered to idols is wrong, not because of the meat itself, but because of the implied endorsement of the idolatry. Thus, Paul's interpretation does not conflict with Acts 15 but actually implies a very strict interpretation, by which eating kosher meat would also be forbidden, if the meat were falsely advertised as having been offered to an idol.

In Yochanan (John) 10:22-23 we read:

> Now the Feast of Chanukkah was held

---

[1] "things offered to idols" Greek: ελδωλοθυτος which also appears in the Greek New Testament in Acts 15:29; 21:25; 1Cor. 8:1, 4, 7, 10; 10:19 aned Rev. 2:14, 20.

> in Yerushalayim and it was winter. And
> Yeshua was walking in the Temple, in the
> porch of Shlomo.

Now this gives some context to the surrounding events. For example, in Yoch. 10:11-18 Yeshua speaks of laying his life down. A major aspect of Channukah was celebration of martys in the days of the Maccabees who laid their lives down for Torah and for Israel.

In Yoch. 10:24 the Judeans want Yeshua to reveal to them whether or not he is the Messiah. According to 1Maccabees 4:46, upon building a new alter the people took the stones from the profanes alter and not knowing what to do with them they stored them "in a convenient place on the Temple mount" until a prophet would come and tell them what to do with the stones. The Judeans were pressing Yeshua to prove he was Messiah by telling them what to do with the profaned stones. Yeshua's answer did not satisfy them. They took up these very stones preparing to stone Yeshua with them (Yoch. 10:31) accusing him of again committing and abomination of desolation (Yoch. 10:33).

ספר מקבים א
1Maccabim

CHAPTER 1

1 And it happened, after that Alexander son of Philip, the Macedonian, who came out of the land of Chettiim, had smitten Darius king of the Persians and Medes, that he reigned in his stead, the first over Greece,

2 And made many wars, and won many strong holds, and slew the kings of the earth,

3 And went through to the ends of the earth, and took spoils of many nations, insomuch that the earth was quiet before him; whereupon he was exalted and his heart was lifted up.

4 And he gathered a mighty strong host and ruled over countries, and nations, and kings, who became tributaries unto him.

5 And after these things he fell sick, and perceived that he should die.

6 Wherefore he called his servants, such as were honourable, and had been brought up with him from his youth, and parted his kingdom among them, while he was yet alive.

7 So Alexander reigned twelves years, and then died.

8 And his servants bare rule every one in his place.

9 And after his death they all put crowns upon themselves; so did their sons after them many years: and evils were multiplied in the earth.

10 And there came out of them a wicked root Antiochus surnamed Epiphanes, son of Antiochus the king, who had been an hostage at Rome, and he reigned in the hundred and thirty and seventh year of the kingdom of the Greeks.

11 In those days went there out of Yisrael those who opposed the Torah[2], who persuaded many, saying, Let us go and make a covenant with the heathen that are round about us: for since we departed from them we have had much sorrow.

12 So this device pleased them well.

---

[2] "those who opposed the Torah" Greek: παρανομοι "opposers of Torah" from the Greek prefix παρα "to oppose" and the Greek word νομος "Torah". Aramaic: אנשא בני עולא "men [who were] sons of wickedness"

13 Then certain of the people were so forward herein, that they went to the king, who gave them licence to do after the ordinances of the heathen:

14 Whereupon they built a place of exercise at Yerushalayim according to the customs of the heathen:

15 And made themselves uncircumcised[3], and forsook the set-apart covenant, and joined themselves to the heathen, and were sold to do mischief.

16 Now when the kingdom was established before Antiochus, he thought to reign over Egypt that he might have the dominion of two realms.

17 Wherefore he entered into Egypt with a great multitude, with chariots, and elephants, and horsemen, and a great navy,

18 And made war against Ptolomy king of Egypt: but Ptolomy was afraid of him, and fled; and many were wounded to death.

19 Thus they got the strong cities in the land of Egypt and he took the spoils thereof.

20 And after that Antiochus had smitten Egypt, he returned again in the hundred forty and third year, and went up against Yisrael and Yerushalayim with a great multitude,

21 And entered proudly into the sanctuary, and took away the golden altar, and the menorah of light, and all the vessels thereof,

22 And the table of the shewbread, and the pouring vessels, and the vials. and the censers of gold, and the veil, and the crown, and the golden ornaments that were before the Temple, all which he pulled off.

23 He took also the silver and the gold, and the precious vessels: also he took the hidden treasures which he found.

24 And when he had taken all away, he went into his own land, having made a great massacre, and spoken very proudly.

25 Therefore there was a great mourning in Yisrael, in every place where they were;

26 So that the princes and elders mourned, the virgins and young men were made feeble, and the beauty of women was changed.

27 Every bridegroom took up lamentation, and she that sat in the marriage chamber was in heaviness,

28 The land also was moved for the inhabitants thereof, and all the house of Ya'akov was covered with confusion.

29 And after two years fully expired the king sent his chief collector of tribute unto the cities of Y'hudah, who came unto Yerushalayim with a great multitude,

---

[3] 1Cor. 7:18; m.Avot 3:11

30 And spake peaceable words unto them, but all was deceit: for when they had given him credence, he fell suddenly upon the city, and smote it very sore, and destroyed much people of Yisrael.

31 And when he had taken the spoils of the city, he set it on fire, and pulled down the houses and walls thereof on every side.

32 But the women and children took they captive, and possessed the cattle.

33 Then builded they the city of David with a great and strong wall, and with mighty towers, and made it a strong hold for them.

34 And they put therein a sinful nation[4], men opposed to the Torah[5], and fortified themselves therein.

35 They stored it also with armour and victuals, and when they had gathered together the spoils of Yerushalayim, they laid them up there, and so they became a sore snare:

36 For it was a place to lie in wait against the sanctuary, and an evil adversary to Yisrael.

37 Thus they shed innocent blood on every side of the sanctuary, and defiled it:

38 Insomuch that the inhabitants of Yerushalayim fled because of them: whereupon the city was made an habitation of strangers, and became strange to those that were born in her; and her own children left her.

39 Her sanctuary was laid waste like a wilderness, her feasts were turned into mourning, her sabbaths into reproach her honour into contempt.

40 As had been her glory, so was her dishonour increased, and her excellency was turned into mourning.

41 Moreover king Antiochus wrote to his whole kingdom, that all should be one people,

42 And every one should leave his laws: so all the heathen agreed according to the commandment of the king.

43 Yes, many also of the Israelites consented to his religion, and sacrificed unto idols, and profaned the sabbath.

44 For the king had sent letters by messengers unto Yerushalayim and the cities of Y'hudah that they should follow the strange laws of the land,

45 And forbid burnt offerings, and sacrifice, and drink offerings, in the Temple; and that they should profane the sabbaths and festival days:

---

[4] or "sinful gentiles" compare Gal. 2:15 and Tobit 13:6
[5] Greek: παρανομοι "opposers of Torah" See note to 1Macc. 111

46 And pollute the sanctuary and set-apart people:

47 Set up altars, and groves, and chapels of idols, and sacrifice swine's flesh, and unclean beasts:

48 That they should also leave their children uncircumcised, and make their souls abominable with all manner of uncleanness and profanation:

49 To the end they might forget the Torah, and change all the ordinances.

50 And whosoever would not do according to the commandment of the king, he said, he should die.

51 In the selfsame manner wrote he to his whole kingdom, and appointed overseers over all the people, commanding the cities of Y'hudah to sacrifice, city by city.

52 Then many of the people were gathered unto them, to wit every one that forsook the Torah; and so they committed evils in the land;

53 And drove the Israelites into secret places, even wheresoever they could flee for succour.

54 Now the fifteenth day of the month Kislev, in the hundred forty and fifth year, they set up the abomination of desolation[6] upon the altar, and built idol altars throughout the cities of Y'hudah on every side;

55 And burnt incense at the doors of their houses, and in the streets.

56 And when they had rent in pieces the books of the Torah which they found, they burnt them with fire.

57 And whosoever was found with any the Book of the Testament, or if any committed to the Torah, the king's commandment was, that they should put him to death.

58 Thus did they by their authority unto the Israelites every month, to as many as were found in the cities.

59 Now the five and twentieth day of the month they did sacrifice upon the idol altar[7], which was upon the altar of Elohim.

60 At which time according to the commandment they put to death certain women, that had caused their children to be circumcised.

61 And they hung the infants about their necks, and rifled their houses, and slew them that had circumcised them.

62 Howbeit many in Yisrael were fully resolved and confirmed in themselves not to eat any unclean thing.

---

[6] Dan. 9:27; 11:31; 12:11; 2Macc. 6:2; Mt. 24:15; Mk. 13:14
[7] 2Macc. 6:4-5

63 Wherefore the rather to die, that they might not be defiled with meats, and that they might not profane the set-apart covenant: so then they died[8].

64 And there was very great wrath upon Yisrael.

CHAPTER 2

1 In those days arose Mattityahu the son of Yochanan, the son of Shim'on, a cohen of the sons of Yahuariv, from Yerushalayim, and dwelt in Modin.

2 And he had five sons, Yochanan, called Gaddi[9]:

3 Shim'on; called Tarasi[10]:

4 Y'hudah, who was called Maccabee[11]:

5 El'azar, called Kharon: and Yahunatan, whose surname was Khafos[12].

6 And when he saw the blasphemies that were committed in Y'hudah and Yerushalayim,

7 He said, Woe is me! wherefore was I born to see this misery of my people, and of the set-apart city, and to dwell there, when it was delivered into the hand of the enemy, and the sanctuary into the hand of strangers?

8 Her Temple is become as a man without glory.

9 Her glorious vessels are carried away into captivity, her infants are slain in the streets, her young men with the sword of the enemy.

10 What nation has not had a part in her kingdom and gotten of her spoils?

11 All her ornaments are taken away; of a free woman she is become a bondslave.

12 And, behold, our sanctuary, even our beauty and our glory, is laid waste, and the Goyim have profaned it.

13 To what end therefore shall we live any longer?

14 Then Mattityahu and his sons rent their clothes, and put on sackcloth, and mourned very sore.

---

[8] 2Macc. 6-7; 4Macc.

[9] Aramaic: גדי "Gadi" "a Gadite" or "the fortunate". The Greek has mistransliterated this as Καδδις "Kaddis"

[10] Aramaic: תרסי "fighter" The Greek has mistransliterated: Θασσι "Thassi"

[11] Aramaic: מקבי "the hammer"

[12] Aramaic: חפוס "the digger"

15 In the mean while the king's officers, such as compelled the people to revolt, came into the city Modin, to make them sacrifice.

16 And when many of Yisrael came unto them, Mattityahu also and his sons came together.

17 Then answered the king's officers, and said to Mattityahu on this wise, You are a ruler, and an honourable and great man in this city, and strengthened with sons and brothers:

18 Now therefore come you first, and fulfil the king's commandment, like as all the heathen have done, yea, and the men of Y'hudah also, and such as remain at Yerushalayim: so shall you and your house be in the number of the king's friends, and you and your children shall be honoured with silver and gold, and many rewards.

19 Then Mattityahu answered and spake with a loud voice, Though all the nations that are under the king's dominion obey him, and fall away every one from the religion of their fathers, and give consent to his commandments:

20 Yet will I and my sons and my brothers walk in the covenant of our fathers.

21 Elohim forbid that we should forsake the Torah and the ordinances.

22 We will not hearken to the king's words, to go from our religion, either on the right hand, or the left.

23 Now when he had left speaking these words, there came one of the Y'hudim in the sight of all to sacrifice on the altar which was at Modin, according to the king's commandment.

24 Which thing when Mattityahu saw, he was inflamed with zeal, and his reins trembled, neither could he forbear to show his anger according to judgment: wherefore he ran, and slew him upon the altar.

25 Also the king's commissioner, who compelled men to sacrifice, he killed at that time, and the altar he pulled down.

26 Thus dealt he zealously for the Torah of Elohim like as Pinchas did unto Zambri the son of Shalom[13].

27 And Mattityahu cried throughout the city with a loud voice, saying, Whosoever is zealous of the Torah, and maintains the covenant, let him follow me.

28 So he and his sons fled into the mountains, and left all that ever they had in the city[14].

29 Then many that sought after justice and judgment went down into the wilderness, to dwell there:

---

[13] Num. 256-15; 1Macc. 254
[14] Heb. 1137; 2Macc. 527

30 Both they, and their children, and their wives; and their cattle; because afflictions increased sore upon them.

31 Now when it was told the king's servants, and the host that was at Yerushalayim, in the city of David, that certain men, who had broken the king's commandment, were gone down into the secret places in the wilderness,

32 They pursued after them a great number, and having overtaken them, they camped against them, and made war against them on the sabbath day.

33 And they said unto them, Let that which you have done hitherto suffice; come forth, and do according to the commandment of the king, and you shall live.

34 But they said, We will not come forth, neither will we do the king's commandment, to profane the sabbath day.

35 So then they gave them the battle with all speed.

36 Howbeit they answered them not, neither cast they a stone at them, nor stopped the places where they lay hid;

37 But said, Let us die all in our innocency: heaven and earth will testify for us, that you put us to death wrongfully.

38 So they rose up against them in battle on the sabbath, and they slew them, with their wives and children and their cattle, to the number of a thousand people.

39 Now when Mattityahu and his friends understood hereof, they mourned for them right sore.

40 And one of them said to another, If we all do as our brothers have done, and fight not for our lives and laws against the heathen, they will now quickly root us out of the earth.

41 At that time therefore they decreed, saying, Whosoever shall come to make battle with us on the sabbath day, we will fight against him; neither will we die all, as our brothers that were murdered in the secret places.

42 Then came there unto him a company of Chasidim who were mighty men of Yisrael, even all such as were voluntarily devoted unto the Torah.

43 Also all they that fled for persecution joined themselves unto them, and were a stay unto them.

44 So they joined their forces, and smote sinful men in their anger, and wicked men in their wrath: but the rest fled to the heathen for succour.

45 Then Mattityahu and his friends went round about, and pulled down the altars:

46 And what children soever they found within the coast of Yisrael uncircumcised, those they circumcised valiantly.

47 They pursued also after the proud men, and the work prospered in their hand.

48 So they recovered the Torah out of the hand of the Goyim, and out of the hand of kings, neither suffered they the sinner to triumph.

49 Now when the time drew near that Mattityahu should die, he said unto his sons, Now has pride and rebuke gotten strength, and the time of destruction, and the wrath of indignation:

50 Now therefore, my sons, be you zealous for the Torah, and give your lives for the covenant of your fathers.

51 Call to remembrance what acts our fathers did in their time; so shall you receive great honour and an everlasting name.

52 Was not Avraham found faithful in temptation, and it was imputed unto him for righteousness[15]?

53 Yosef in the time of his distress kept the commandment and was made master of Egypt[16].

54 Pinchas our father in being zealous and fervent obtained the covenant of an everlasting priesthood[17].

55 Yahushua[18] for fulfilling the word was made a judge in Yisrael[19].

56 Kalev for bearing witness before the congregation[20] received the heritage of the land[21].

57 David for being merciful possessed the throne of an everlasting kingdom[22].

58 Eliyahu for being zealous and fervent for the Torah was taken up into heaven[23].

59 Hananyah, 'Azaryah, and Misha'el, by believing were saved out of the flame[24].

60 Daniel in his uprightness[25] was delivered from the mouth of lions[26].

61 And thus consider you throughout all ages, that none that put their trust in him shall be overcome.

---

[15] Gen. 15:6; Gen. 22:15-18; James 2:21-23; Rom. 4:3; Gal. 3:6

[16] Gen. 39-45

[17] Num. 25:6-15; 1Macc. 2:26

[18] Aramaic: ישוע "Yeshua" Greek: Ιησους These are used in Aramaic and Greek for both the names Yeshua and Yahushua (Joshua).

[19] Josh. 11-9

[20] Num. 13:6, 30; 14:6-38

[21] Num. 26:65; 32:12; Deut. 1:36

[22] 2Sam. 7:16; Ps. 89:35-37

[23] 2Kn. 2:11-12

[24] Dan. 11:9; 38-30

[25] "in his uprightness"; Aramaic: בפשיטותה Greek: απλοτητι

[26] Dan. 6:1-24

62 Fear not then the words of a sinful man: for his glory shall be dung and worms.

63 Today he shall be lifted up and tomorrow he shall not be found, because he is returned into his dust, and his thought is come to nothing.

64 Wherefore, you my sons, be valiant and show yourselves men in the behalf of the Torah; for by it shall you obtain glory.

65 And behold, I know that your brother Shim'on is a man of counsel, give ear unto him always: he shall be a father unto you.

66 As for Y'hudah Maccabee, he has been mighty and strong, even from his youth up: let him be your captain, and fight the battle of the people.

67 Take also unto you all those that observe the Torah, and avenge you the wrong of your people.

68 Recompense fully the heathen, and take heed to the commandments of the Torah.

69 So he blessed them, and was gathered to his fathers.

70 And he died in the hundred forty and sixth year, and his sons buried him in the sepulchres of his fathers at Modin, and all Yisrael made great lamentation for him.

CHAPTER 3

1 Then his son Y'hudah, called Maccabee, rose up in his stead.

2 And all his brothers helped him, and so did all they that held with his father, and they fought with cheerfulness the battle of Yisrael.

3 So he gat his people great honour, and put on a breastplate as a giant, and girt his warlike harness about him, and he made battles, protecting the host with his sword.

4 In his acts he was like a lion, and like a lion's whelp roaring for his prey.

5 For He pursued the wicked, and sought them out, and burnt up those that vexed his people.

6 Wherefore the wicked shrunk for fear of him, and all the workers of iniquity were troubled, because salvation prospered in his hand.

7 He grieved also many kings, and made Ya'akov glad with his acts, and his memorial is blessed for ever.

8 Moreover he went through the cities of Y'hudah, destroying the ungodly out of them, and turning away wrath from Yisrael:

9 So that he was renowned unto the utmost part of the earth, and he received unto him such as were ready to perish.

10 Then Apollonius gathered the Goyim together, and a great host out of Samaria, to fight against Yisrael.

11 Which thing when Y'hudah perceived, he went forth to meet him, and so he smote him, and slew him: many also fell down slain, but the rest fled.

12 Wherefore Y'hudah took their spoils, and Apollonius' sword also, and therewith he fought all his life long.

13 Now when Seron, a prince of the army of Syria, heard say that Y'hudah had gathered unto him a multitude and company of the faithful to go out with him to war;

14 He said, I will get me a name and honour in the kingdom; for I will go fight with Y'hudah and them that are with him, who despise the king's commandment.

15 So he made him ready to go up, and there went with him a mighty host of the ungodly to help him, and to be avenged of the children of Yisrael.

16 And when he came near to the going up of Beit-Haran, Y'hudah went forth to meet him with a small company:

17 Who, when they saw the host coming to meet them, said unto Y'hudah, How shall we be able, being so few, to fight against so great a multitude and so strong, seeing we are ready to faint with fasting all this day?

18 Unto whom Y'hudah answered, It is no hard matter for many to be shut up in the hands of a few; and with the Elohim of heaven it is all one, to deliver with a great multitude, or a small company:

19 For the victory of battle stands not in the multitude of an host; but strength comes from heaven.

20 They come against us in much pride and iniquity to destroy us, and our wives and children, and to spoil us:

21 But we fight for our lives and our laws.

22 And YHWH himself will overthrow them before our face: and as for you, be you not afraid of them.

23 Now as soon as he had left off speaking, he leapt suddenly upon them, and so Seron and his host was overthrown before him.

24 And they pursued them from the going down of Beit-Haran unto the plain, where were slain about eight hundred men of them; and the residue fled into the land of the Philistines.

25 Then began the fear of Y'hudah and his brothers, and an exceeding great dread, to fall upon the nations round about them:

26 Insomuch as his fame came unto the king, and all nations talked of the battles of Y'hudah.

27 Now when king Antiochus heard these things, he was full of indignation: wherefore he sent and gathered together all the forces of his realm, even a very strong army.

28 He opened also his treasure, and gave his soldiers pay for a year, commanding them to be ready whensoever he should need them.

29 Nevertheless, when he saw that the money of his treasures failed and that the tributes in the country were small, because of the dissension and plague, which he had brought upon the land in taking away the laws which had been of old time;

30 He feared that he should not be able to bear the charges any longer, nor to have such gifts to give so liberally as he did before: for he had abounded above the kings that were before him.

31 Wherefore, being greatly perplexed in his mind, he determined to go into Persia, there to take the tributes of the countries, and to gather much money.

32 So he left Lysias, a nobleman, and one of the blood royal, to oversee the affairs of the king from the river Euphrates unto the borders of Egypt:

33 And to bring up his son Antiochus, until he came again.

34 Moreover he delivered unto him the half of his forces, and the elephants, and gave him charge of all things that he would have done, as also concerning them that dwelt in Y'hudah and Yerushalayim:

35 To wit, that he should send an army against them, to destroy and root out the strength of Yisrael, and the remnant of Yerushalayim, and to take away their memorial from that place;

36 And that he should place strangers in all their quarters, and divide their land by lot.

37 So the king took the half of the forces that remained, and departed from Antioch, his royal city, the hundred forty and seventh year; and having passed the river Euphrates, he went through the high countries.

38 Then Lysias chose Ptolomy the son of Dorymenes, Nicanor, and Gorgias, mighty men of the king's friends:

39 And with them he sent forty thousand footmen, and seven thousand horsemen, to go into the land of Y'hudah, and to destroy it, as the king commanded.

40 So they went forth with all their power, and came and pitched by Emmaus in the plain country.

41 And the merchants of the country, hearing the fame of them, took silver and gold very much, with servants, and came into the camp to buy the children of Yisrael for slaves: a power also of Syria and of the land of the Philistines joined themselves unto them.

42 Now when Y'hudah and his brothers saw that miseries were multiplied, and that the forces did encamp themselves in their borders: for they knew how the king had given commandment to destroy the people, and utterly abolish them;

43 They said one to another, Let us restore the decayed fortune of our people, and let us fight for our people and the sanctuary.

44 Then was the congregation gathered together, that they might be ready for battle, and that they might pray, and ask mercy and compassion.

45 Now Yerushalayim lay void as a wilderness, there was none of her children that went in or out: the sanctuary also was trodden down, and aliens kept the strong hold; the heathen had their habitation in that place; and joy was taken from Ya'akov, and the pipe with the harp ceased.

46 Wherefore the Israelites assembled themselves together, and came to Mitzpah, over against Yerushalayim; for in Mitzpah was the place where they prayed aforetime in Yisrael.

47 Then they fasted that day, and put on sackcloth, and cast ashes upon their heads, and rent their clothes,

48 And laid open the Book of the Torah, wherein the heathen had sought to paint the likeness of their images.

49 They brought also the cohenim's garments, and the firstfruits, and the tithes: and the Nazarites[27] they stirred up, who had accomplished their days.

50 Then cried they with a loud voice toward heaven, saying, What shall we do with these, and whither shall we carry them away?

51 For your sanctuary is trodden down and profaned, and your cohenim are in heaviness, and brought low.

52 And lo, the heathen are assembled together against us to destroy us: what things they imagine against us, you know.

53 How shall we be able to stand against them, except you, O Elohim, be our help?

54 Then sounded they with trumpets, and cried with a loud voice.

55 And after this Y'hudah ordained captains over the people, even captains over thousands, and over hundreds, and over fifties, and over tens.

56 But as for such as were building houses, or had betrothed wives, or were planting vineyards, or were fearful, those he commanded that

---

[27] Num. 6:1-21

they should return, every man to his own house, according to the Torah[28].

57 So the camp removed, and pitched upon the south side of Emmaus.

58 And Y'hudah said, arm yourselves, and be valiant men, and see that you be in readiness against the morning, that you may fight with these nations, that are assembled together against us to destroy us and our sanctuary:

59 For it is better for us to die in battle, than to behold the calamities of our people and our sanctuary.

60 Nevertheless, as the will of Elohim is in heaven, so let him do.

CHAPTER 4

1 Then took Gorgias five thousand footmen, and a thousand of the best horsemen, and removed out of the camp by night;

2 To the end he might rush in upon the camp of the Y'hudim, and smite them suddenly. And the men of the fortress were his guides.

3 Now when Y'hudah heard thereof he himself removed, and the valiant men with him, that he might smite the king's army which was at Emmaus,

4 While as yet the forces were dispersed from the camp.

5 In the mean season came Gorgias by night into the camp of Y'hudah: and when he found no man there, he sought them in the mountains: for said he, These fellows flee from us

6 But as soon as it was day, Y'hudah showed himself in the plain with three thousand men, who nevertheless had neither armour nor swords to their minds.

7 And they saw the camp of the heathen, that it was strong and well harnessed, and compassed round about with horsemen; and these were expert of war.

8 Then said Y'hudah to the men that were with him, Fear you not their multitude, neither be you afraid of their assault.

9 Remember how our fathers were delivered in the Red Sea, when Pharaoh pursued them with an army. [29]

10 Now therefore let us cry unto heaven, if peradventure YHWH will have mercy upon us, and remember the covenant of our fathers, and destroy this host before our face this day:

---

[28] Deut. 20:5-8
[29] Ex. 14:21-29

11 That so all the heathen may know that there is one who delivers and saves Yisrael.

12 Then the strangers lifted up their eyes, and saw them coming over against them.

13 Wherefore they went out of the camp to battle; but they that were with Y'hudah sounded their trumpets.

14 So they joined battle, and the heathen being discomfited fled into the plain.

15 Howbeit all the hindmost of them were slain with the sword: for they pursued them unto Gazera, and unto the plains of Idumea, and Azotus, and Jamnia, so that there were slain of them upon a three thousand men.

16 This done, Y'hudah returned again with his host from pursuing them,

17 And said to the people, Be not greedy of the spoil inasmuch as there is a battle before us,

18 And Gorgias and his host are here by us in the mountain: but stand you now against our enemies, and overcome them, and after this you may boldly take the spoils.

19 As Y'hudah was yet speaking these words, there appeared a part of them looking out of the mountain:

20 Who when they perceived that the Y'hudim had put their host to flight and were burning the tents; for the smoke that was seen declared what was done:

21 When therefore they perceived these things, they were sore afraid, and seeing also the host of Y'hudah in the plain ready to fight,

22 They fled every one into the land of strangers.

23 Then Y'hudah returned to spoil the tents, where they got much gold, and silver, and blue silk, and purple of the sea, and great riches.

24 After this they went home, and sung a song of thanksgiving, and praised YHWH in heaven: because it is good, because his mercy endures forever.

25 Thus Yisrael had a great deliverance that day.

26 Now all the strangers that had escaped came and told Lysias what had happened:

27 Who, when he heard thereof, was confounded and discouraged, because neither such things as he would were done unto Yisrael, nor such things as the king commanded him were come to pass.

28 The next year therefore following Lysias gathered together threescore thousand choice men of foot, and five thousand horsemen, that he might subdue them.

29 So they came into Idumea, and pitched their tents at Beit-Tzur, and Y'hudah met them with ten thousand men.

30 And when he saw that mighty army, he prayed and said, Blessed are you, O Saviour of Yisrael, who did quell the violence of the mighty man by the hand of your servant David, and gavs the host of strangers into the hands of Yahunatan the son of Shaul, and his armourbearer;

31 Shut up this army in the hand of your people Yisrael, and let them be confounded in their power and horsemen:

32 Make them to be of no courage, and cause the boldness of their strength to fall away, and let them quake at their destruction:

33 Cast them down with the sword of them that love you, and let all those that know your name praise you with thanksgiving.

34 So they joined battle; and there were slain of the host of Lysias about five thousand men, even before them were they slain.

35 Now when Lysias saw his army put to flight, and the manliness of Y'hudah' soldiers, and how they were ready either to live or die valiantly, he went into Antiochia, and gathered together a company of strangers, and having made his army greater than it was, he purposed to come again into Y'hudah.

36 Then said Y'hudah and his brothers, Behold, our enemies are discomfited: let us go up to cleanse and dedicate the sanctuary.

37 Upon this all the host assembled themselves together, and went up into mount Tzion.

38 And when they saw the sanctuary desolate, and the altar profaned, and the gates burned up, and shrubs growing in the courts as in a forest, or in one of the mountains, yea, and the cohenim' chambers pulled down;

39 They rent their clothes, and made great lamentation, and cast ashes upon their heads,

40 And fell down flat to the ground upon their faces, and blew an alarm with the trumpets, and cried toward heaven.

41 Then Y'hudah appointed certain men to fight against those that were in the fortress, until he had cleansed the sanctuary.

42 So he chose cohenim of blameless conversation, such as had pleasure in the Torah:

43 Who cleansed the sanctuary, and bare out the defiled stones into an unclean place.

44 And when as they consulted what to do with the altar of burnt offerings, which was profaned;

45 They thought it best to pull it down, lest it should be a reproach to them, because the heathen had defiled it: wherefore they pulled it down,

46 And laid up the stones in the mountain of the Temple in a convenient place, until there should come a prophet to show what should be done with them[30].

47 Then they took whole stones according to the Torah[31], and built a new altar according to the former;

48 And made up the sanctuary, and the things that were within the Temple, and hallowed the courts.

49 They made also new set-apart vessels, and into the Temple they brought the menorah, and the altar of burnt offerings, and of incense, and the table.

50 And upon the altar they burned incense, and the lamps that were upon the menorah they lit, that they might give light in the Temple[32].

51 Furthermore they set the loaves upon the table[33], and spread out the veils, and finished all the works which they had begun to make.

52 Now on the five and twentieth day of the ninth month, which is called the month Kislev, in the hundred forty and eighth year, they rose up betimes in the morning,

53 And offered sacrifice according to the Torah upon the new altar of burnt offerings, which they had made.

54 Look, at what time and what day the heathen had profaned it, even in that was it dedicated with songs, and citherns, and harps, and cymbals.

55 Then all the people fell upon their faces, worshipping and praising the Elohim of heaven, who had given them good success.

56 And so they kept the dedication of the altar eight days and offered burnt offerings with gladness, and sacrificed the sacrifice of deliverance and praise.

57 They decked also the forefront of the Temple with crowns of gold, and with shields; and the gates and the chambers they renewed, and hanged doors upon them.

58 Thus was there very great gladness among the people, for that the reproach of the heathen was put away.

59 Moreover Y'hudah and his brothers with the whole congregation of Yisrael ordained, that the days of the dedication of the altar should be

---

[30] John 1022-24
[31] Ex. 20:25; Deut. 27:5-6
[32] Ex. 30:7-8
[33] Ex. 25:30

kept in their season from year to year by the space of eight days, from the five and twentieth day of the month Kislev, with mirth and gladness[34].

60 At that time also they builded up the mount Tzion with high walls and strong towers round about, lest the Goyim should come and tread it down as they had done before.

61 And they set there a garrison to keep it, and fortified Beit-Tzur to preserve it; that the people might have a defence against Idumea.

CHAPTER 5

1 Now when the nations round about heard that the altar was built and the sanctuary renewed as before, it displeased them very much.

2 Wherefore they thought to destroy the generation of Ya'akov that was among them, and thereupon they began to slay and destroy the people.

3 Then Y'hudah fought against the children of Esau in Idumea at Akrabattene, because they besieged Yisrael: and he gave them a great overthrow, and abated their courage, and took their spoils.

4 Also he remembered the injury of the children of Be'on[35], who had been a snare and an offence unto the people, in that they lay in wait for them in the ways.

5 He shut them up therefore in the towers, and encamped against them, and destroyed them utterly, and burned the towers of that place with fire, and all that were therein.

6 Afterward he passed over to the children of Ammon, where he found a mighty power, and much people, with Timotheus their captain.

7 So he fought many battles with them, till at length they were discomfited before him; and he smote them.

8 And when he had taken Ya'zer[36], with the towns belonging thereto, he returned into Y'hudah.

9 Then the heathen that were at Gil'ad assembled themselves together against the Israelites that were in their quarters, to destroy them; but they fled to the fortress of Dathema.

10 And sent letters unto Y'hudah and his brothers, The heathen that are round about us are assembled together against us to destroy us:

---

[34] 2Macc. 10:1-9; John 10:22; b.Shabb. 21b
[35] Num. 32:3
[36] Num. 32:3

11 And they are preparing to come and take the fortress whereunto we are fled, Timotheus being captain of their host.

12 Come now therefore, and deliver us from their hands, for many of us are slain:

13 Yes, all our brothers that were in the places of Tobie are put to death: their wives and their children also they have carried away captives, and borne away their stuff; and they have destroyed there about a thousand men.

14 While these letters were yet reading, behold, there came other messengers from Galil with their clothes rent, who reported on this wise,

15 And said, They of Ptolemais, and of Tzor, and Tzidon, and all Galil of the Goyim[37], are assembled together against us to consume us.

16 Now when Y'hudah and the people heard these words, there assembled a great congregation together, to consult what they should do for their brothers, that were in trouble, and assaulted of them.

17 Then said Y'hudah unto Shim'on his brother, Choose you out men, and go and deliver your brothers that are in Galil, for I and Yahunatan my brother will go into the country of Gil'ad.

18 So he left Yosef the son of Z'kharyah, and Azaryah, captains of the people, with the remnant of the host in Y'hudah to keep it.

19 Unto whom he gave commandment, saying, Take you the charge of this people, and see that you make not war against the heathen until the time that we come again.

20 Now unto Shim'on were given three thousand men to go into Galil, and unto Y'hudah eight thousand men for the country of Gil'ad.

21 Then went Shim'on into Galil, where he fought many battles with the heathen, so that the heathen were discomfited by him.

22 And he pursued them unto the gate of Ptolemais; and there were slain of the heathen about three thousand men, whose spoils he took.

23 And those that were in Galil, and in Arbatta, with their wives and their children, and all that they had, took he away with him, and brought them into Y'hudah with great joy.

24 Y'hudah Maccabee also and his brother Yahunatan went over Yardan, and travelled three days' journey in the wilderness,

25 Where they met with the Nabateans, who came unto them in a peaceable manner, and told them every thing that had happened to their brothers in the land of Gil'ad:

---

[37] Is. 9:1; Mt. 4:15

26 And how that many of them were shut up in Bosora, and Bosor, and Alema, Casphor, Maked, and Carnaim; all these cities are strong and great:

27 And that they were shut up in the rest of the cities of the country of Gil'ad, and that against to morrow they had appointed to bring their host against the forts, and to take them, and to destroy them all in one day.

28 Hereupon Y'hudah and his host turned suddenly by the way of the wilderness unto Bosora; and when he had won the city, he slew all the males with the edge of the sword, and took all their spoils, and burned the city with fire,

29 From whence he removed by night, and went till he came to the fortress.

30 And betimes in the morning they looked up, and, behold, there was an innumerable people bearing ladders and other engines of war, to take the fortress: for they assaulted them.

31 When Y'hudah therefore saw that the battle was begun, and that the cry of the city went up to heaven, with trumpets, and a great sound,

32 He said unto his host, Fight this day for your brothers.

33 So he went forth behind them in three companies, who sounded their trumpets, and cried with prayer.

34 Then the host of Timotheus, knowing that it was Maccabee, fled from him: wherefore he smote them with a great slaughter; so that there were killed of them that day about eight thousand men.

35 This done, Y'hudah turned aside to Mitzpah; and after he had assaulted it he took and slew all the males therein, and received the spoils thereof and and burnt it with fire.

36 From thence went he, and took Casphon, Maked, Bosor, and the other cities of the country of Gil'ad.

37 After these things gathered Timotheus another host and encamped against Raphon beyond the brook.

38 So Y'hudah sent men to espy the host, who brought him word, saying, All the heathen that be round about us are assembled unto them, even a very great host.

39 He has also hired the Arabians to help them and they have pitched their tents beyond the brook, ready to come and fight against you. Upon this Y'hudah went to meet them.

40 Then Timotheus said unto the captains of his host, When Y'hudah and his host come near the brook, if he pass over first unto us, we shall not be able to withstand him; for he will mightily prevail against us:

41 But if he be afraid, and camp beyond the river, we shall go over unto him, and prevail against him.

42 Now when Y'hudah came near the brook, he caused the scribes of the people to remain by the brook: unto whom he gave commandment, saying, Suffer no man to remain in the camp, but let all come to the battle.

43 So he went first over unto them, and all the people after him: then all the heathen, being discomfited before him, cast away their weapons, and fled unto the Temple that was at Carnaim.

44 But they took the city, and burned the Temple with all that were therein. Thus was Carnaim subdued, neither could they stand any longer before Y'hudah.

45 Then Y'hudah gathered together all the Israelites that were in the country of Gil'ad, from the least unto the greatest, even their wives, and their children, and their stuff, a very great host, to the end they might come into the land of Y'hudah.

46 Now when they came unto Ephron, (this was a great city in the way as they should go, very well fortified) they could not turn from it, either on the right hand or the left, but must needs pass through the midst of it.

47 Then they of the city shut them out, and stopped up the gates with stones.

48 Whereupon Y'hudah sent unto them in peaceable manner, saying, Let us pass through your land to go into our own country, and none shall do you any hurt; we will only pass through on foot: howbeit they would not open unto him.

49 Wherefore Y'hudah commanded a proclamation to be made throughout the host, that every man should pitch his tent in the place where he was.

50 So the soldiers pitched, and assaulted the city all that day and all that night, till at the length the city was delivered into his hands:

51 Who then slew all the males with the edge of the sword, and rased the city, and took the spoils thereof, and passed through the city over them that were slain[38].

52 After this went they over Yardan into the great plain before Bethsan.

53 And Y'hudah gathered together those that came behind, and exhorted the people all the way through, till they came into the land of Y'hudah.

54 So they went up to mount Tzion with joy and gladness, where they offered burnt offerings, because not one of them were slain until they had returned in peace.

---

[38] Num. 21:21-24

55 Now what time as Y'hudah and Yahunatan were in the land of Gil'ad, and Shim'on his brother in Galil before Ptolemais,

56 Yosef the son of Zacharias, and 'Azaryah, captains of the garrisons, heard of the valiant acts and warlike deeds which they had done.

57 Wherefore they said, Let us also get us a name, and go fight against the heathen that are round about us.

58 So when they had given charge unto the garrison that was with them, they went toward Jamnia.

59 Then came Gorgias and his men out of the city to fight against them.

60 And so it was, that Yosef and Azaras were put to flight, and pursued unto the borders of Y'hudah: and there were slain that day of the people of Yisrael about two thousand men.

61 Thus was there a great overthrow among the children of Yisrael, because they were not obedient unto Y'hudah and his brothers, but thought to do some valiant act.

62 Moreover these men came not of the seed of those, by whose hand deliverance was given unto Yisrael.

63 Howbeit the man Y'hudah and his brothers were greatly renowned in the sight of all Yisrael, and of all the heathen, wheresoever their name was heard of;

64 Insomuch as the the people assembled unto them with joyful acclamations.

65 Afterward went Y'hudah forth with his brothers, and fought against the children of Esau in the land toward the south, where he smote Hebron, and the towns thereof, and pulled down the fortress of it, and burned the towers thereof round about.

66 From thence he removed to go into the land of the Philistines, and passed through Samaria.

67 At that time certain cohenim, desirous to show their valour, were slain in battle, for that they went out to fight unadvisedly.

68 So Y'hudah turned to Azotus in the land of the Philistines, and when he had pulled down their altars, and burned their carved images with fire, and spoiled their cities, he returned into the land of Y'hudah.

CHAPTER 6

1 About that time king Antiochus travelling through the high countries heard say, that Elymais in the country of Persia was a city greatly renowned for riches, silver, and gold;

2 And that there was in it a very rich temple, wherein were coverings of gold, and breastplates, and shields, which Alexander, son of Philip, the Macedonian king, who reigned first among the Greeks, had left there.

3 Wherefore he came and sought to take the city, and to spoil it; but he was not able, because they of the city, having had warning thereof,

4 Rose up against him in battle: so he fled, and departed thence with great heaviness, and returned to Babylon.

5 Moreover there came one who brought him tidings into Persia, that the armies, which went against the land of Y'hudah, were put to flight:

6 And that Lysias, who went forth first with a great power was driven away of the Y'hudim; and that they were made strong by the armour, and power, and store of spoils, which they had gotten of the armies, whom they had destroyed:

7 Also that they had pulled down the abomination, which he had set up upon the altar in Yerushalayim, and that they had compassed about the sanctuary with high walls, as before, and his city Beit-Tzur.

8 Now when the king heard these words, he was astonished and sore moved: whereupon he laid him down upon his bed, and fell sick for grief, because it had not befallen him as he looked for.

9 And there he continued many days: for his grief was ever more and more, and he made account that he should die.

10 Wherefore he called for all his friends, and said unto them, The sleep is gone from mine eyes, and my heart fails for very care.

11 And I thought with myself, Into what tribulation am I come, and how great a flood of misery is it, wherein now I am! for I was bountiful and beloved in my power.

12 But now I remember the evils that I did at Yerushalayim, and that I took all the vessels of gold and silver that were therein, and sent to destroy the inhabitants of Y'hudah without a cause.

13 I perceive therefore that for this cause these troubles are come upon me, and, behold, I perish through great grief in a strange land.

14 Then called he for Philip, one of his friends, who he made ruler over all his realm,

15 And gave him the crown, and his robe, and his signet, to the end he should bring up his son Antiochus, and nourish him up for the kingdom.

16 So king Antiochus died there in the hundred forty and ninth year.

17 Now when Lysias knew that the king was dead, he set up Antiochus his son, whom he had brought up being young, to reign in his stead, and his name he called Eupator.

18 About this time they that were in the tower shut up the Israelites round about the sanctuary, and sought always their hurt, and the strengthening of the heathen.

19 Wherefore Y'hudah, purposing to destroy them, called all the people together to besiege them.

20 So they came together, and besieged them in the hundred and fiftieth year, and he made mounts for shot against them, and other engines.

21 Howbeit certain of them that were besieged got forth, unto whom some ungodly men of Yisrael joined themselves:

22 And they went unto the king, and said, How long will it be ere you execute judgment, and avenge our brothers?

23 We have been willing to serve your father, and to do as he would have us, and to obey his commandments;

24 For which cause they of our nation besiege the tower, and are alienated from us: moreover as many of us as they could light on they slew, and spoiled our inheritance.

25 Neither have they stretched out their hand against us only, but also against their borders.

26 And, behold, this day are they besieging the tower at Yerushalayim, to take it: the sanctuary also and Beit-Tzur have they fortified.

27 Wherefore if you dost not prevent them quickly, they will do the greater things than these, neither shall you be able to rule them.

28 Now when the king heard this, he was angry, and gathered together all his friends, and the captains of his army, and those that had charge of the horse.

29 There came also unto him from other kingdoms, and from isles of the sea, bands of hired soldiers.

30 So that the number of his army was an hundred thousand footmen, and twenty thousand horsemen, and two and thirty elephants exercised in battle.

31 These went through Idumea, and pitched against Beit-Tzur, which they assaulted many days, making engines of war; but they of Beit-Tzur came out, and burned them with fire, and fought valiantly.

32 Upon this Y'hudah removed from the tower, and pitched in Beit-Z'kharyah, over against the king's camp.

33 Then the king rising very early marched fiercely with his host toward Beit-Z'kharyah, where his armies made them ready to battle, and sounded the trumpets.

34 And to the end they might provoke the elephants to fight, they showed them the blood of grapes and mulberries.

35 Moreover they divided the beasts among the armies, and for every elephant they appointed a thousand men, armed with coats of mail, and with helmets of brass on their heads; and beside this, for every beast were ordained five hundred horsemen of the best.

36 These were ready at every occasion: wheresoever the beast was, and whithersoever the beast went, they went also, neither departed they from him.

37 And upon the beasts were there strong towers of wood, which covered every one of them, and were girt fast unto them with devices: there were also upon every one two and thirty strong men, that fought upon them, beside the Indian that ruled him.

38 As for the remnant of the horsemen, they set them on this side and that side at the two parts of the host giving them signs what to do, and being harnessed all over amidst the ranks.

39 Now when the sun shone upon the shields of gold and brass, the mountains glistered therewith, and shined like lamps of fire.

40 So part of the king's army being spread upon the high mountains, and part on the valleys below, they marched on safely and in order.

41 Wherefore all that heard the noise of their multitude, and the marching of the company, and the rattling of the harness, were moved: for the army was very great and mighty.

42 Then Y'hudah and his host drew near, and entered into battle, and there were slain of the king's army six hundred men.

43 El'azar also, surnamed Savaran, perceiving that one of the beasts, armed with royal harness, was higher than all the rest, and supposing that the king was upon him,

44 Put himself in jeopardy, to the end he might deliver his people, and get him a perpetual name:

45 Wherefore he ran upon him courageously through the midst of the battle, slaying on the right hand and on the left, so that they were divided from him on both sides.

46 Which done, he crept under the elephant, and thrust him under, and slew him: whereupon the elephant fell down upon him, and there he died.

47 Howbeit the rest of the Y'hudim seeing the strength of the king, and the violence of his forces, turned away from them.

48 Then the king's army went up to Yerushalayim to meet them, and the king pitched his tents against Y'hudah, and against mount Tzion.

49 But with them that were in Beit-Tzur he made peace: for they came out of the city, because they had no victuals there to endure the siege, it being a year of rest to the land[39].

50 So the king took Beit-Tzur, and set a garrison there to keep it.

51 As for the sanctuary, he besieged it many days: and set there artillery with engines and instruments to cast fire and stones, and pieces to cast darts and slings.

52 Whereupon they also made engines against their engines, and held them battle a long season.

53 Yet at the last, their vessels being without victuals, (for that it was the seventh year, and they in Y'hudah that were delivered from the Goyim, had eaten up the residue of the store;)

54 There were but a few left in the sanctuary, because the famine did so prevail against them, that they were fain to disperse themselves, every man to his own place.

55 At that time Lysias heard say, that Philip, whom Antiochus the king, whiles he lived, had appointed to bring up his son Antiochus, that he might be king,

56 Was returned out of Persia and Media, and the king's host also that went with him, and that he sought to take unto him the ruling of the affairs.

57 Wherefore he went in all haste, and said to the king and the captains of the host and the company, We decay daily, and our victuals are but small, and the place we lay siege unto is strong, and the affairs of the kingdom lie upon us:

58 Now therefore let us be friends with these men, and make peace with them, and with all their nation;

59 And covenant with them, that they shall live after their laws, as they did before: for they are therefore displeased, and have done all these things, because we abolished their laws.

60 So the king and the princes were content: wherefore he sent unto them to make peace; and they accepted thereof.

61 Also the king and the princes made an oath unto them: whereupon they went out of the strong hold.

62 Then the king entered into mount Tzion; but when he saw the strength of the place, he broke his oath that he had made, and gave commandment to pull down the wall round about.

63 Afterward departed he in all haste, and returned unto Antiochia, where he found Philip to be master of the city: so he fought against him, and took the city by force.

---

[39] Ex. 23:11; Lev. 25:3-7

CHAPTER 7

1 In the hundred and one and fiftieth year Demetrius the son of Seleucus departed from Rome, and came up with a few men unto a city of the sea coast, and reigned there.

2 And as he entered into the palace of his ancestors, so it was, that his forces had taken Antiochus and Lysias, to bring them unto him.

3 Wherefore, when he knew it, he said, Let me not see their faces.

4 So his host slew them. Now when Demetrius was set upon the throne of his kingdom,

5 There came unto him all the wicked and ungodly men of Yisrael, having Alcimus, who was desirous to be Cohen HaGadol, for their captain:

6 And they accused the people to the king, saying, Y'hudah and his brothers have slain all your friends, and driven us out of our own land.

7 Now therefore send some man whom you trust, and let him go and see what havoc he has made among us, and in the king's land, and let him punish them with all them that aid them.

8 Then the king chose Bacchides, a friend of the king, who ruled beyond the flood, and was a great man in the kingdom, and faithful to the king,

9 And him he sent with that wicked Alcimus, whom he made Cohen HaGadol, and commanded that he should take vengeance of the children of Yisrael.

10 So they departed, and came with a great power into the land of Y'hudah, where they sent messengers to Y'hudah and his brothers with peaceable words deceitfully.

11 But they gave no heed to their words; for they saw that they were come with a great power.

12 Then did there assemble unto Alcimus and Bacchides a company of scribes, to require justice.

13 Now the Chasidim were the first among the children of Yisrael that sought peace of them:

14 For said they, One that is a cohen of the seed of Aharon is come with this army, and he will do us no wrong.

15 So he spake unto them, peaceably, and sware unto them, saying, we will procure the harm neither of you nor your friends.

16 Whereupon they believed him: howbeit he took of them threescore men, and slew them in one day, according to the words which he wrote,

17 The flesh of your set-apart-ones have they cast out, and their blood have they shed round about Yerushalayim, and there was none to bury them.

18 Wherefore the fear and dread of them fell upon all the people, who said, There is neither truth nor righteousness in them; for they have broken the covenant and oath that they made.

19 After this, removed Bacchides from Yerushalayim, and pitched his tents in Beit-Zada, where he sent and took many of the men that had forsaken him, and certain of the people also, and when he had slain them, he cast them into the great pit.

20 Then committed he the country to Alcimus, and left with him a power to aid him: so Bacchides went to the king.

21 But Alcimus contended for the Cohen HaGadolhood.

22 And unto him resorted all such as troubled the people, who, after they had gotten the land of Y'hudah into their power, did much hurt in Yisrael.

23 Now when Y'hudah saw all the mischief that Alcimus and his company had done among the Israelites, even above the heathen,

24 He went out into all the coasts of Y'hudah round about, and took vengeance of them that had revolted from him, so that they durst no more go forth into the country.

25 On the other side, when Alcimus saw that Y'hudah and his company had gotten the upper hand, and knew that he was not able to abide their force, he went again to the king, and said all the worst of them that he could.

26 Then the king sent Nicanor, one of his honourable princes, a man that bare deadly hate unto Yisrael, with commandment to destroy the people.

27 So Nicanor came to Yerushalayim with a great force; and sent unto Y'hudah and his brothers deceitfully with friendly words, saying,

28 Let there be no battle between me and you; I will come with a few men, that I may see you in peace.

29 He came therefore to Y'hudah, and they saluted one another peaceably. Howbeit the enemies were prepared to take away Y'hudah by violence.

30 Which thing after it was known to Y'hudah, to wit, that he came unto him with deceit, he was sore afraid of him, and would see his face no more.

31 Nicanor also, when he saw that his counsel was discovered, went out to fight against Y'hudah beside K'far-Shlama:

32 Where there were slain of Nicanor's side about five thousand men, and the rest fled into the city of David.

33 After this went Nicanor up to mount Tzion, and there came out of the sanctuary certain of the cohenim and certain of the elders of the people, to salute him peaceably, and to show him the burnt sacrifice that was offered for the king.

34 But he mocked them, and laughed at them, and abused them shamefully, and spake proudly,

35 And sware in his wrath, saying, Unless Y'hudah and his host be now delivered into my hands, if ever I come again in safety, I will burn up this house: and with that he went out in a great rage.

36 Then the cohenim entered in, and stood before the altar and the Temple, weeping, and saying,

37 You, O YHWH, did choose this house to be called by your name, and to be a house of prayer and petition for your people:

38 Be avenged of this man and his host, and let them fall by the sword: remember their blasphemies, and suffer them not to continue any longer.

39 So Nicanor went out of Yerushalayim, and pitched his tents in Beit-Haran, where an host out of Syria met him.

40 But Y'hudah pitched in Adasa with three thousand men, and there he prayed, saying,

41 O YHWH, when they that were sent from the king of the Assyrians blasphemed, your angel went out, and smote an hundred fourscore and five thousand of them.

42 Even so destroy you this host before us this day, that the rest may know that he has spoken blasphemously against your sanctuary, and judge you him according to his wickedness.

43 So the thirteenth day of the month Adar the hosts joined battle: but Nicanor's host was discomfited, and he himself was first slain in the battle.

44 Now when Nicanor's host saw that he was slain, they cast away their weapons, and fled.

45 Then they pursued after them a day's journey, from Adasa unto Gazera, sounding an alarm after them with their trumpets.

46 Whereupon they came forth out of all the towns of Y'hudah round about, and closed them in; so that they, turning back upon them that pursued them, were all slain with the sword, and not one of them was left.

47 Afterwards they took the spoils, and the prey, and smote off Nicanors head, and his right hand, which he stretched out so proudly, and brought them away, and hanged them up toward Yerushalayim.

48 For this cause the people rejoiced greatly, and they kept that day a day of great gladness.

49 Moreover they ordained to keep yearly this day, being the thirteenth of Adar.

50 Thus the land of Y'hudah was in rest a little while.

CHAPTER 8

1 Now Y'hudah had heard of the the Romans, that they were mighty and valiant men, and such as would lovingly accept all that joined themselves unto them, and make a league of amity with all that came unto them;

2 And that they were men of great valour. It was told him also of their wars and noble acts which they had done among the Galatians, and how they had conquered them, and brought them under tribute;

3 And what they had done in the country of Spain, for the winning of the mines of the silver and gold which is there;

4 And that by their policy and patience they had conquered all the place, though it were very far from them; and the kings also that came against them from the uttermost part of the earth, till they had discomfited them, and given them a great overthrow, so that the rest did give them tribute every year:

5 Beside this, how they had discomfited in battle Philip, and Perseus, king of the Citims, with others that lifted up themselves against them, and had overcome them:

6 How also Antiochus the great king of Asia, that came against them in battle, having an hundred and twenty elephants, with horsemen, and chariots, and a very great army, was discomfited by them;

7 And how they took him alive, and covenanted that he and such as reigned after him should pay a great tribute, and give hostages, and that which was agreed upon,

8 And the country of India, and Media and Lydia and of the best countries, which they took of him, and gave to king Eumenes:

9 Moreover how the Greeks had determined to come and destroy them;

10 And that they, having knowledge thereof sent against them a certain captain, and fighting with them slew many of them, and carried away captives their wives and their children, and spoiled them, and took possession of their lands, and pulled down their strong holds, and brought them to be their servants unto this day:

11 It was told him besides, how they destroyed and brought under their dominion all other kingdoms and isles that at any time resisted them;

12 But with their friends and such as relied upon them they kept amity: and that they had conquered kingdoms both far and nigh, insomuch as all that heard of their name were afraid of them:

13 Also that, whom they would help to a kingdom, those reign; and whom again they would, they displace: finally, that they were greatly exalted:

14 Yet for all this none of them wore a crown or was clothed in purple, to be magnified thereby:

15 Moreover how they had made for themselves a senate house, wherein three hundred and twenty men sat in council daily, consulting alway for the people, to the end they might be well ordered:

16 And that they committed their government to one man every year, who ruled over all their country, and that all were obedient to that one, and that there was neither envy nor emmulation among them.

17 In consideration of these things, Y'hudah chose Eupolemus the son of Yochanan, the son of Accos, and Jason the son of El'azar, and sent them to Rome, to make a league of amity and confederacy with them,

18 And to intreat them that they would take the yoke from them; for they saw that the kingdom of the Greeks did oppress Yisrael with servitude.

19 They went therefore to Rome, which was a very great journey, and came into the senate, where they spake and said.

20 Y'hudah Maccabee with his brothers, and the people of the Y'hudim, have sent us unto you, to make a confederacy and peace with you, and that we might be registered your confederates and friends.

21 So that matter pleased the Romans well.

22 And this is the copy of the epistle which the senate wrote back again in tables of brass, and sent to Yerushalayim, that there they might have by them a memorial of peace and confederacy:

23 Good success be to the Romans, and to the people of the Y'hudim, by sea and by land for ever: the sword also and enemy be far from them,

24 If there come first any war upon the Romans or any of their confederates throughout all their dominion,

25 The people of the Y'hudim shall help them, as the time shall be appointed, with all their heart:

26 Neither shall they give any thing unto them that make war upon them, or aid them with victuals, weapons, money, or ships, as it has seemed good unto the Romans; but they shall keep their covenants without taking any thing therefore.

27 In the same manner also, if war come first upon the nation of the Y'hudim, the Romans shall help them with all their heart, according as the time shall be appointed them:

28 Neither shall victuals be given to them that take part against them, or weapons, or money, or ships, as it has seemed good to the Romans; but they shall keep their covenants, and that without deceit.

29 According to these articles did the Romans make a covenant with the people of the Y'hudim.

30 Howbeit if hereafter the one party or the other shall think to meet to add or diminish any thing, they may do it at their pleasures, and whatsoever they shall add or take away shall be ratified.

31 And as touching the evils that Demetrius does to the Y'hudim, we have written unto him, saying, Wherefore you made your yoke heavy upon our friends and confederates the Y'hudim?

32 If therefore they complain any more against you, we will do them justice, and fight with you by sea and by land.

CHAPTER 9

1 Furthermore, when Demetrius heard the Nicanor and his host were slain in battle, he sent Bacchides and Alcimus into the land of Y'hudah the second time, and with them the chief strength of his host:

2 Who went forth by the way that leads to Galgala, and pitched their tents before Masaloth, which is in Arbela, and after they had won it, they slew much people.

3 Also the first month of the hundred fifty and second year they encamped before Yerushalayim:

4 From whence they removed, and went to Berea, with twenty thousand footmen and two thousand horsemen.

5 Now Y'hudah had pitched his tents at Eleasa, and three thousand chosen men with him:

6 Who seeing the multitude of the other army to he so great were sore afraid; whereupon many conveyed themselves out of the host, insomuch as abode of them no more but eight hundred men.

7 When Y'hudah therefore saw that his host slipt away, and that the battle pressed upon him, he was sore troubled in mind, and much distressed, for that he had no time to gather them together.

8 Nevertheless unto them that remained he said, Let us arise and go up against our enemies, if peradventure we may be able to fight with them.

9 But they dehorted him, saying, We shall never be able: let us now rather save our lives, and hereafter we will return with our brothers, and fight against them: for we are but few.

10 Then Y'hudah said, Elohim forbid that I should do this thing, and flee away from them: if our time be come, let us die manfully for our brothers, and let us not stain our honour.

11 With that the host of Bacchides removed out of their tents, and stood over against them, their horsemen being divided into two troops, and their slingers and archers going before the host and they that marched in the foreward were all mighty men.

12 As for Bacchides, he was in the right wing: so the host drew near on the two parts, and sounded their trumpets.

13 They also of Y'hudah' side, even they sounded their trumpets also, so that the earth shook at the noise of the armies, and the battle continued from morning till night.

14 Now when Y'hudah perceived that Bacchides and the strength of his army were on the right side, he took with him all the hardy men,

15 Who discomfited the right wing, and pursued them unto the mount Azotus.

16 But when they of the left wing saw that they of the right wing were discomfited, they followed upon Y'hudah and those that were with him hard at the heels from behind:

17 Whereupon there was a sore battle, insomuch as many were slain on both parts.

18 Y'hudah also was killed, and the remnant fled.

19 Then Yahunatan and Shim'on took Y'hudah their brother, and buried him in the sepulchre of his fathers in Modin.

20 Moreover they bewailed him, and all Yisrael made great lamentation for him, and mourned many days, saying,

21 How is the valiant man fallen, that delivered Yisrael![40]

22 As for the other things concerning Y'hudah and his wars, and the noble acts which he did, and his greatness, they are not written: for they were very many.

23 Now after the death of Y'hudah the wicked began to put forth their heads in all the coasts of Yisrael, and there arose up all such as wrought iniquity.

24 In those days also was there a very great famine, by reason whereof the country revolted, and went with them.

25 Then Bacchides chose the wicked men, and made them masters of the country.

---

[40] 2Sam. 1:19

26 And they made enquiry and search for Y'hudah' friends, and brought them unto Bacchides, who took vengeance of them, and used them despitefully.

27 So was there a great affliction in Yisrael, the like whereof was not since the time that a prophet was not seen among them.

28 For this cause all Y'hudah' friends came together, and said unto Yahunatan,

29 Since your brother Y'hudah died, we have no man like him to go forth against our enemies, and Bacchides, and against them of our nation that are adversaries to us.

30 Now therefore we have chosen you this day to be our prince and captain in his stead, that you may fight our battles.

31 Upon this Yahunatan took the governance upon him at that time, and rose up instead of his brother Y'hudah.

32 But when Bacchides gat knowledge thereof, he sought for to slay him

33 Then Yahunatan, and Shim'on his brother, and all that were with him, perceiving that, fled into the wilderness of Tekoa, and pitched their tents by the water of the pool Asphar.

34 Which when Bacchides understood, he came near to Yardan with all his host upon the sabbath day.

35 Now Yahunatan had sent his brother Yochanan, a captain of the people, to pray his friends the Nabathites, that they might leave with them their carriage, which was much.

36 But the children of Jambri came out of Medaba, and took Yochanan, and all that he had, and went their way with it.

37 After this came word to Yahunatan and Shim'on his brother, that the children of Jambri made a great marriage, and were bringing the bride from Nadabatha with a great train, as being the daughter of one of the great princes of Chanaan.

38 Therefore they remembered Yochanan their brother, and went up, and hid themselves under the covert of the mountain:

39 Where they lifted up their eyes, and looked, and, behold, there was much ado and great carriage: and the bridegroom came forth, and his friends and brothers, to meet them with drums, and instruments of music, and many weapons.

40 Then Yahunatan and they that were with him rose up against them from the place where they lay in ambush, and made a slaughter of them in such sort, as many fell down dead, and the remnant fled into the mountain, and they took all their spoils.

41 Thus was the marriage turned into mourning, and the noise of their melody into lamentation.

42 So when they had avenged fully the blood of their brother, they turned again to the marsh of Yardan.

43 Now when Bacchides heard hereof, he came on the sabbath day unto the banks of Yardan with a great power.

44 Then Yahunatan said to his company, Let us go up now and fight for our lives, for it stands not with us to day, as in time past:

45 For, behold, the battle is before us and behind us, and the water of Yardan on this side and that side, the marsh likewise and wood, neither is there place for us to turn aside.

46 Wherefore cry you now unto heaven, that you may be delivered from the hand of your enemies.

47 With that they joined battle, and Yahunatan stretched forth his hand to smite Bacchides, but he turned back from him.

48 Then Yahunatan and they that were with him leapt into Yardan, and swam over unto the other bank: howbeit the other passed not over Yardan unto them.

49 So there were slain of Bacchides' side that day about a thousand men.

50 Afterward returned Bacchides to Yerushalayim and repaired the strong cites in Y'hudah; the fort in Yericho, and Emmaus, and Beit-Haran, and Beit-El, and Timnat, Pharathoni, and Taphon, these did he strengthen with high walls, with gates and with bars.

51 And in them he set a garrison, that they might work malice upon Yisrael.

52 He fortified also the city Beit-Tzur, and Gazera, and the tower, and put forces in them, and provision of victuals.

53 Besides, he took the chief men's sons in the country for hostages, and put them into the tower at Yerushalayim to be kept.

54 Moreover in the hundred fifty and third year, in the second month, Alcimus commanded that the wall of the inner court of the sanctuary should be pulled down; he pulled down also the works of the prophets

55 And as he began to pull down, even at that time was Alcimus plagued, and his enterprizes hindered: for his mouth was stopped, and he was taken with a palsy, so that he could no more speak any thing, nor give order concerning his house.

56 So Alcimus died at that time with great torment.

57 Now when Bacchides saw that Alcimus was dead, he returned to the king: whereupon the land of Y'hudah was in rest two years.

58 Then all the ungodly men held a council, saying, Behold, Yahunatan and his company are at ease, and dwell without care: now therefore we will bring Bacchides hither, who shall take them all in one night.

59 So they went and consulted with him.

60 Then removed he, and came with a great host, and sent letters privily to his adherents in Y'hudah, that they should take Yahunatan and those that were with him: howbeit they could not, because their counsel was known unto them.

61 Wherefore they took of the men of the country, that were authors of that mischief, about fifty persons, and slew them.

62 Afterward Yahunatan, and Shim'on, and they that were with him, got them away to Bethbasi, which is in the wilderness, and they repaired the decays thereof, and made it strong.

63 Which thing when Bacchides knew, he gathered together all his host, and sent word to them that were of Y'hudah.

64 Then went he and laid siege against Bethbasi; and they fought against it a long season and made engines of war.

65 But Yahunatan left his brother Shim'on in the city, and went forth himself into the country, and with a certain number went he forth.

66 And he smote Odonarkes and his brothers, and the children of Phasiron in their tent.

67 And when he began to smite them, and came up with his forces, Shim'on and his company went out of the city, and burned up the engines of war,

68 And fought against Bacchides, who was discomfited by them, and they afflicted him sore: for his counsel and travail was in vain.

69 Wherefore he was very wroth at the wicked men that gave him counsel to come into the country, inasmuch as he slew many of them, and purposed to return into his own country.

70 Whereof when Yahunatan had knowledge, he sent ambassadors unto him, to the end he should make peace with him, and deliver them the prisoners.

71 Which thing he accepted, and did according to his demands, and sware unto him that he would never do him harm all the days of his life.

72 When therefore he had restored unto him the prisoners that he had taken aforetime out of the land of Y'hudah, he returned and went his way into his own land, neither came he any more into their borders.

73 Thus the sword ceased from Yisrael: but Yahunatan dwelt at Machmas, and began to govern the people; and he destroyed the ungodly men out of Yisrael.

CHAPTER 10

1 In the hundred and sixtieth year Alexander, the son of Antiochus surnamed Epiphanes, went up and took Ptolemais: for the people had received him, by means whereof he reigned there,

2 Now when king Demetrius heard thereof, he gathered together an exceeding great host, and went forth against him to fight.

3 Moreover Demetrius sent letters unto Yahunatan with loving words, so as he magnified him.

4 For said he, Let us first make peace with him, before he join with Alexander against us:

5 Else he will remember all the evils that we have done against him, and against his brothers and his people.

6 Wherefore he gave him authority to gather together an host, and to provide weapons, that he might aid him in battle: he commanded also that the hostages that were in the tower should be delivered him.

7 Then came Yahunatan to Yerushalayim, and read the letters in the audience of all the people, and of them that were in the tower:

8 Who were sore afraid, when they heard that the king had given him authority to gather together an host.

9 Whereupon they of the tower delivered their hostages unto Yahunatan, and he delivered them unto their parents.

10 This done, Yahunatan settled himself in Yerushalayim, and began to build and repair the city.

11 And he commanded the workmen to build the walls and the mount Tzion and about with square stones for fortification; and they did so.

12 Then the strangers, that were in the fortresses which Bacchides had built, fled away;

13 Insomuch as every man left his place, and went into his own country.

14 Only at Beit-Tzur certain of those that had forsaken the Torah and the commandments remained still: for it was their place of refuge.

15 Now when king Alexander had heard what promises Demetrius had sent unto Yahunatan: when also it was told him of the battles and noble acts which he and his brothers had done, and of the pains that they had endured,

16 He said, Shall we find such another man? now therefore we will make him our friend and confederate.

17 Upon this he wrote a letter, and sent it unto him, according to these words, saying,

18 King Alexander to his brother Yahunatan sends greeting:

19 We have heard of you, that you are a man of great power, and meet to be our friend.

20 Wherefore now this day we ordain you to be the Cohen HaGadol of your nation, and to be called the king's friend; (and therewithal he sent him a purple robe and a crown of gold:) and require you to take our part, and keep friendship with us.

21 So in the seventh month of the hundred and sixtieth year, at the feast of the Sukkot, Yahunatan put on the set-apart robe[41], and gathered together forces, and provided much armour.

22 Whereof when Demetrius heard, he was very sorry, and said,

23 What have we done, that Alexander has prevented us in making amity with the Y'hudim to strengthen himself?

24 I also will write unto them words of encouragement, and promise them dignities and gifts, that I may have their aid.

25 He sent unto them therefore to this effect: King Demetrius unto the people of the Y'hudim sends greeting:

26 Whereas you have kept covenants with us, and continued in our friendship, not joining yourselves with our enemies, we have heard hereof, and are glad.

27 Wherefore now continue you still to be faithful unto us, and we will well recompense you for the things you do in our behalf,

28 And will grant you many immunities, and give you rewards.

29 And now do I free you, and for your sake I release all the Y'hudim, from tributes, and from the customs of salt, and from crown taxes,

30 And from that which appertains unto me to receive for the third part or the seed, and the half of the fruit of the trees, I release it from this day forth, so that they shall not be taken of the land of Y'hudah, nor of the three governments which are added thereunto out of the country of Samaria and Galil, from this day forth for evermore.

31 Let Yerushalayim also be set-apart and free, with the borders thereof, both from tenths and tributes.

32 And as for the tower which is at Yerushalayim, I yield up authority over it, and give the Cohen HaGadol, that he may set in it such men as he shall choose to keep it.

33 Moreover I freely set at liberty every one of the Y'hudim, that were carried captives out of the land of Y'hudah into any part of my kingdom, and I will that all my officers remit the tributes even of their cattle.

34 Furthermore I will that all the feasts, and sabbaths, and new moons, and solemn days, and the three days before the feast, and the three

---

[41] Ex. 28:1-39; 39:1-26

days after the feast shall be all of immunity and freedom for all the Y'hudim in my realm.

35 Also no man shall have authority to meddle with or to molest any of them in any matter.

36 I will further, that there be enrolled among the king's forces about thirty thousand men of the Y'hudim, unto whom pay shall be given, as belongs to all king's forces.

37 And of them some shall be placed in the king's strong holds, of whom also some shall be set over the affairs of the kingdom, which are of trust: and I will that their overseers and governors be of themselves, and that they live after their own laws, even as the king has commanded in the land of Y'hudah.

38 And concerning the three governments that are added to Y'hudah from the country of Samaria, let them be joined with Y'hudah, that they may be reckoned to be under one, nor bound to obey other authority than the Cohen HaGadol's.

39 As for Ptolemais, and the land pertaining thereto, I give it as a free gift to the sanctuary at Yerushalayim for the necessary expences of the sanctuary.

40 Moreover I give every year fifteen thousand shekels of silver out of the king's accounts from the places appertaining.

41 And all the overplus, which the officers payed not in as in former time, from henceforth shall be given toward the works of the Temple.

42 And beside this, the five thousand shekels of silver, which they took from the uses of the Temple out of the accounts year by year, even those things shall be released, because they appertain to the cohenim that minister.

43 And whosoever they be that flee unto the Temple at Yerushalayim, or be within the liberties hereof, being indebted unto the king, or for any other matter, let them be at liberty, and all that they have in my realm.

44 For the building also and repairing of the works of the sanctuary expences shall be given of the king's accounts.

45 Yes, and for the building of the walls of Yerushalayim, and the fortifying thereof round about, expences shall be given out of the king's accounts, as also for the building of the walls in Y'hudah.

46 Now when Yahunatan and the people heard these words, they gave no credit unto them, nor received them, because they remembered the great evil that he had done in Yisrael; for he had afflicted them very sore.

47 But with Alexander they were well pleased, because he was the first that entreated of true peace with them, and they were confederate with him always.

48 Then gathered king Alexander great forces, and camped over against Demetrius.

49 And after the two kings had joined battle, Demetrius' host fled: but Alexander followed after him, and prevailed against them.

50 And he continued the battle very sore until the sun went down: and that day was Demetrius slain.

51 Afterward Alexander sent ambassadors to Ptolomy king of Egypt with a message to this effect:

52 Forasmuch as I am come again to my realm, and am set in the throne of my progenitors, and have gotten the dominion, and overthrown Demetrius, and recovered our country;

53 For after I had joined battle with him, both he and his host was discomfited by us, so that we sit in the throne of his kingdom:

54 Now therefore let us make a league of amity together, and give me now your daughter to wife: and I will be your son in law, and will give both you and her as according to your dignity.

55 Then Ptolomy the king gave answer, saying, Happy be the day wherein you did return into the land of your fathers, and sat in the throne of their kingdom.

56 And now will I do to you, as you have written: meet me therefore at Ptolemais, that we may see one another; for I will marry my daughter to you according to your desire.

57 So Ptolomy went out of Egypt with his daughter Cleopatra, and they came unto Ptolemais in the hundred threescore and second year:

58 Where king Alexander meeting him, he gave unto him his daughter Cleopatra, and celebrated her marriage at Ptolemais with great glory, as the manner of kings is.

59 Now king Alexander had written unto Yahunatan, that he should come and meet him.

60 Who thereupon went honourably to Ptolemais, where he met the two kings, and gave them and their friends silver and gold, and many presents, and found favour in their sight.

61 At that time certain pestilent fellows of Yisrael, men of a wicked life, assembled themselves against him, to accuse him: but the king would not hear them.

62 Yes more than that, the king commanded to take off his garments, and clothe him in purple: and they did so.

63 And he made him sit by himself, and said into his princes, Go with him into the midst of the city, and make proclamation, that no man

complain against him of any matter, and that no man trouble him for any manner of cause.

64 Now when his accusers saw that he was honored according to the proclamation, and clothed in purple, they fled all away.

65 So the king honoured him, and wrote him among his chief friends, and made him a duke, and partaker of his dominion.

66 Afterward Yahunatan returned to Yerushalayim with peace and gladness.

67 Furthermore in the; hundred threescore and fifth year came Demetrius son of Demetrius out of Crete into the land of his fathers:

68 Whereof when king Alexander heard tell, he was right sorry, and returned into Antioch.

69 Then Demetrius made Apollonius the governor of Celosyria his general, who gathered together a great host, and camped in Jamnia, and sent unto Yahunatan the Cohen HaGadol, saying,

70 You alone lift up thyself against us, and I am laughed to scorn for your sake, and reproached: and why dost you vaunt your power against us in the mountains?

71 Now therefore, if you trust in your own strength, come down to us into the plain field, and there let us try the matter together: for with me is the power of the cities.

72 Ask and learn who I am, and the rest that take our part, and they shall tell you that your foot is not able to to flight in their own land.

73 Wherefore now you shall not be able to abide the horsemen and so great a power in the plain, where is neither stone nor flint, nor place to flee unto.

74 So when Yahunatan heard these words of Apollonius, he was moved in his mind, and choosing ten thousand men he went out of Yerushalayim, where Shim'on his brother met him for to help him.

75 And he pitched his tents against Yafa: but; they of Yafa shut him out of the city, because Apollonius had a garrison there.

76 Then Yahunatan laid siege unto it: whereupon they of the city let him in for fear: and so Yahunatan won Yafa.

77 Whereof when Apollonius heard, he took three thousand horsemen, with a great host of footmen, and went to Azotus as one that journeyed, and therewithal drew him forth into the plain. because he had a great number of horsemen, in whom he put his trust.

78 Then Yahunatan followed after him to Azotus, where the armies joined battle.

79 Now Apollonius had left a thousand horsemen in ambush.

80 And Yahunatan knew that there was an ambushment behind him; for they had compassed in his host, and cast darts at the people, from morning till evening.

81 But the people stood still, as Yahunatan had commanded them: and so the enemies' horses were tired.

82 Then brought Shim'on forth his host, and set them against the footmen, (for the horsemen were spent) who were discomfited by him, and fled.

83 The horsemen also, being scattered in the field, fled to Azotus, and went into Bethdagon, their idol's temple, for safety.

84 But Yahunatan set fire on Azotus, and the cities round about it, and took their spoils; and the Temple of Dagon, with them that were fled into it, he burned with fire.

85 Thus there were burned and slain with the sword well nigh eight thousand men.

86 And from thence Yahunatan removed his host, and camped against Ascalon, where the men of the city came forth, and met him with great pomp.

87 After this returned Yahunatan and his host unto Yerushalayim, having any spoils.

88 Now when king Alexander heard these things, he honoured Yahunatan yet more.

89 And sent him a buckle of gold, as the use is to be given to such as are of the king's blood: he gave him also Accaron with the borders thereof in possession.

CHAPTER 11

1 And the king of Egypt gathered together a great host, like the sand that lies upon the sea shore, and many ships, and went about through deceit to get Alexander's kingdom, and join it to his own.

2 Whereupon he took his journey into Spain in peaceable manner, so as they of the cities opened unto him, and met him: for king Alexander had commanded them so to do, because he was his brother in law.

3 Now as Ptolomy entered into the cities, he set in every one of them a garrison of soldiers to keep it.

4 And when he came near to Azotus, they showed him the Temple of Dagon that was burnt, and Azotus and the suburbs thereof that were destroyed, and the bodies that were cast abroad and them that he had burnt in the battle; for they had made heaps of them by the way where he should pass.

5 Also they told the king whatsoever Yahunatan had done, to the intent he might blame him: but the king held his peace.

6 Then Yahunatan met the king with great pomp at Yafa, where they saluted one another, and lodged.

7 Afterward Yahunatan, when he had gone with the king to the river called Eleutherus, returned again to Yerushalayim.

8 King Ptolomy therefore, having gotten the dominion of the cities by the sea unto Seleucia upon the sea coast, imagined wicked counsels against Alexander.

9 Whereupon he sent ambasadors unto king Demetrius, saying, Come, let us make a league betwixt us, and I will give you my daughter whom Alexander has, and you shall reign in your father's kingdom:

10 For I repent that I gave my daughter unto him, for he sought to slay me.

11 Thus did he slander him, because he was desirous of his kingdom.

12 Wherefore he took his daughter from him, and gave her to Demetrius, and forsook Alexander, so that their hatred was openly known.

13 Then Ptolomy entered into Antioch, where he set two crowns upon his head, the crown of Asia, and of Egypt.

14 In the mean season was king Alexander in Cilicia, because those that dwelt in those parts had revolted from him.

15 But when Alexander heard of this, he came to war against him: whereupon king Ptolomy brought forth his host, and met him with a mighty power, and put him to flight.

16 So Alexander fled into Arabia there to be defended; but king Ptolomy was exalted:

17 For Zabdiel the Arabian took off Alexander's head, and sent it unto Ptolomy.

18 King Ptolomy also died the third day after, and they that were in the strong holds were slain one of another.

19 By this means Demetrius reigned in the hundred threescore and seventh year.

20 At the same time Yahunatan gathered together them that were in Y'hudah to take the tower that was in Yerushalayim: and he made many engines of war against it.

21 Then came ungodly persons, who hated their own people, went unto the king, and told him that Yahunatan besieged the tower,

22 Whereof when he heard, he was angry, and immediately removing, he came to Ptolemais, and wrote unto Yahunatan, that he should not lay siege to the tower, but come and speak with him at Ptolemais in great haste.

23 Nevertheless Yahunatan, when he heard this, commanded to besiege it still: and he chose certain of the elders of Yisrael and the cohenim, and put himself in peril;

24 And took silver and gold, and raiment, and divers presents besides, and went to Ptolemais unto the king, where he found favour in his sight.

25 And though certain ungodly men of the people had made complaints against him,

26 Yet the king entreated him as his predecessors had done before, and promoted him in the sight of all his friends,

27 And confirmed him in the Cohen HaGadolhood, and in all the honours that he had before, and gave him preeminence among his chief friends.

28 Then Yahunatan desired the king, that he would make Y'hudah free from tribute, as also the three governments, with the country of Samaria; and he promised him three hundred talents.

29 So the king consented, and wrote letters unto Yahunatan of all these things after this manner:

30 King Demetrius unto his brother Yahunatan, and unto the nation of the Y'hudim, sends greeting:

31 We send you here a copy of the letter which we did write unto our cousin Lasthenes concerning you, that you might see it.

32 King Demetrius unto his father Lasthenes sends greeting:

33 We are determined to do good to the people of the Y'hudim, who are our friends, and keep covenants with us, because of their good will toward us.

34 Wherefore we have ratified unto them the borders of Y'hudah, with the three governments of Apherema and Lydda and Ramathem, that are added unto Y'hudah from the country of Samaria, and all things appertaining unto them, for all such as do sacrifice in Yerushalayim, instead of the payments which the king received of them yearly aforetime out of the fruits of the earth and of trees.

35 And as for other things that belong unto us, of the tithes and customs pertaining unto us, as also the saltpits, and the crown taxes, which are due unto us, we discharge them of them all for their relief.

36 And nothing hereof shall be revoked from this time forth for ever.

37 Now therefore see that you make a copy of these things, and let it be delivered unto Yahunatan, and set upon the set-apart mount in a conspicuous place.

38 After this, when king Demetrius saw that the land was quiet before him, and that no resistance was made against him, he sent away all his forces, every one to his own place, except certain bands of strangers,

whom he had gathered from the isles of the heathen: wherefore all the forces of his fathers hated him.

39 Moreover there was one Tryphon, that had been of Alexander's part afore, who, seeing that all the host murmured against Demetrius, went to Simalcue the Arabian that brought up Antiochus the young son of Alexander,

40 And lay sore upon him to deliver him this young Antiochus, that he might reign in his father's stead: he told him therefore all that Demetrius had done, and how his men of war were at enmity with him, and there he remained a long season.

41 In the mean time Yahunatan sent unto king Demetrius, that he would cast those of the tower out of Yerushalayim, and those also in the fortresses: for they fought against Yisrael.

42 So Demetrius sent unto Yahunatan, saying, I will not only do this for you and your people, but I will greatly honour you and your nation, if opportunity serve.

43 Now therefore you shall do well, if you send me men to help me; for all my forces are gone from me.

44 Upon this Yahunatan sent him three thousand strong men unto Antioch: and when they came to the king, the king was very glad of their coming.

45 Howbeit they that were of the city gathered themselves together into the midst of the city, to the number of an hundred and twenty thousand men, and would have slain the king.

46 Wherefore the king fled into the court, but they of the city kept the passages of the city, and began to fight.

47 Then the king called to the Y'hudim for help, who came unto him all at once, and dispersing themselves through the city slew that day in the city to the number of an hundred thousand.

48 Also they set fire on the city, and gat many spoils that day, and delivered the king.

49 So when they of the city saw that the Y'hudim had got the city as they would, their courage was abated: wherefore they made supplication to the king, and cried, saying,

50 Grant us peace, and let the Y'hudim cease from assaulting us and the city.

51 With that they cast away their weapons, and made peace; and the Y'hudim were honoured in the sight of the king, and in the sight of all that were in his realm; and they returned to Yerushalayim, having great spoils.

52 So king Demetrius sat on the throne of his kingdom, and the land was quiet before him.

53 Nevertheless he dissembled in all that ever he spake, and estranged himself from Yahunatan, neither rewarded he him according to the benefits which he had received of him, but troubled him very sore.

54 After this returned Tryphon, and with him the young child Antiochus, who reigned, and was crowned.

55 Then there gathered unto him all the men of war, whom Demetrius had put away, and they fought against Demetrius, who turned his back and fled.

56 Moreover Tryphon took the elephants, and won Antioch.

57 At that time young Antiochus wrote unto Yahunatan, saying, I confirm you in the Cohen HaGadolhood, and appoint you ruler over the four governments, and to be one of the king's friends.

58 Upon this he sent him golden vessels to be served in, and gave him leave to drink in gold, and to be clothed in purple, and to wear a golden buckle.

59 His brother Shim'on also he made captain from the place called The ladder of Tyrus unto the borders of Egypt.

60 Then Yahunatan went forth, and passed through the cities beyond the water, and all the forces of Syria gathered themselves unto him for to help him: and when he came to Ascalon, they of the city met him honourably.

61 From whence he went to Gaza, but they of Gaza shut him out; wherefore he laid siege unto it, and burned the suburbs thereof with fire, and spoiled them.

62 Afterward, when they of Gaza made supplication unto Yahunatan, he made peace with them, and took the sons of their chief men for hostages, and sent them to Yerushalayim, and passed through the country unto Damascus.

63 Now when Yahunatan heard that Demetrius' princes were come to Cades, which is in Galil, with a great power, purposing to remove him out of the country,

64 He went to meet them, and left Shim'on his brother in the country.

65 Then Shim'on encamped against Beit-Tzur and fought against it a long season, and shut it up:

66 But they desired to have peace with him, which he granted them, and then put them out from thence, and took the city, and set a garrison in it.

67 As for Yahunatan and his host, they pitched at the water of Gennesar, from whence betimes in the morning they gat them to the plain of Nasor.

68 And, behold, the host of strangers met them in the plain, who, having laid men in ambush for him in the mountains, came themselves over against him.

69 So when they that lay in ambush rose out of their places and joined battle, all that were of Yahunatan's side fled;

70 Insomuch as there was not one of them left, except Mattityahu the son of Absalom, and Y'hudah the son of Calphi, the captains of the host.

71 Then Yahunatan rent his clothes, and cast earth upon his head, and prayed.

72 Afterwards turning again to battle, he put them to flight, and so they ran away.

73 Now when his own men that were fled saw this, they turned again unto him, and with him pursued them to Cades, even unto their own tents, and there they camped.

74 So there were slain of the heathen that day about three thousand men: but Yahunatan returned to Yerushalayim.

CHAPTER 12

1 Now when Yahunatan saw that time served him, he chose certain men, and sent them to Rome, for to confirm and renew the friendship that they had with them.

2 He sent letters also to the Lacedemonians, and to other places, for the same purpose.

3 So they went unto Rome, and entered into the senate, and said, Yahunatan the Cohen HaGadol, and the people of the Y'hudim, sent us unto you, to the end you should renew the friendship, which you had with them, and league, as in former time.

4 Upon this the Romans gave them letters unto the governors of every place that they should bring them into the land of Y'hudah peaceably.

5 And this is the copy of the letters which Yahunatan wrote to the Lacedemonians:

6 Yahunatan the Cohen HaGadol, and the elders of the nation, and the cohenim, and the other of the Y'hudim, unto the Lacedemonians their brothers send greeting:

7 There were letters sent in times past unto Onias the Cohen HaGadol from Darius, who reigned then among you, to signify that you are our brothers, as the copy here underwritten doth specify.

8 At which time Onias entreated the ambassador that was sent honourably, and received the letters, wherein declaration was made of the league and friendship.

9 Therefore we also, albeit we need none of these things, that we have the set-apart books of scripture in our hands to comfort us,

10 Have nevertheless attempted to send unto you for the renewing of brotherhood and friendship, lest we should become strangers unto you altogether: for there is a long time passed since you sent unto us.

11 We therefore at all times without ceasing, both in our feasts, and other convenient days, do remember you in the sacrifices which we offer, and in our prayers, as reason is, and as it becomes us to think upon our brothers:

12 And we are right glad of your honour.

13 As for ourselves, we have had great troubles and wars on every side, forsomuch as the kings that are round about us have fought against us.

14 Howbeit we would not be troublesome unto you, nor to others of our confederates and friends, in these wars:

15 For we have help from heaven that succours us, so as we are delivered from our enemies, and our enemies are brought under foot.

16 For this cause we chose Numenius the son of Antiochus, and Antipater he son of Jason, and sent them unto the Romans, to renew the amity that we had with them, and the former league.

17 We commanded them also to go unto you, and to salute and to deliver you our letters concerning the renewing of our brotherhood.

18 Wherefore now you shall do well to give us an answer thereto.

19 And this is the copy of the letters which Oniares sent.

20 Areus king of the Lacedemonians to Onias the Cohen HaGadol, greeting:

21 It is found in writing, that the Lacedemonians and Y'hudim are brothers, and that they are of the stock of Avraham:

22 Now therefore, since this is come to our knowledge, you shall do well to write unto us of your prosperity.

23 We do write back again to you, that your cattle and goods are our's, and our's are your's We do command therefore our ambassadors to make report unto you on this wise.

24 Now when Yahunatan heard that Demebius' princes were come to fight against him with a greater host than afore,

25 He removed from Yerushalayim, and met them in the land of Amathis: for he gave them no respite to enter his country.

26 He sent spies also unto their tents, who came again, and told him that they were appointed to come upon them in the night season.

27 Wherefore so soon as the sun was down, Yahunatan commanded his men to watch, and to be in arms, that all the night long they might be ready to fight: also he sent forth centinels round about the host.

28 But when the adversaries heard that Yahunatan and his men were ready for battle, they feared, and trembled in their hearts, and they kindled fires in their camp.

29 Howbeit Yahunatan and his company knew it not till the morning: for they saw the lights burning.

30 Then Yahunatan pursued after them, but overtook them not: for they were gone over the river Eleutherus.

31 Wherefore Yahunatan turned to the Arabians, who were called Zabadeans, and smote them, and took their spoils.

32 And removing thence, he came to Damascus, and so passed through all the country,

33 Shim'on also went forth, and passed through the country unto Ascalon, and the holds there adjoining, from whence he turned aside to Yafa, and won it.

34 For he had heard that they would deliver the hold unto them that took Demetrius' part; wherefore he set a garrison there to keep it.

35 After this came Yahunatan home again, and calling the elders of the people together, he consulted with them about building strong holds in Y'hudah,

36 And making the walls of Yerushalayim higher, and raising a great mount between the tower and the city, for to separate it from the city, that so it might be alone, that men might neither sell nor buy in it.

37 Upon this they came together to build up the city, forasmuch as part of the wall toward the brook on the east side was fallen down, and they repaired that which was called Caphenatha.

38 Shim'on also set up Adida in Sephela, and made it strong with gates and bars.

39 Now Tryphon went about to get the kingdom of Asia, and to kill Antiochus the king, that he might set the crown upon his own head.

40 Howbeit he was afraid that Yahunatan would not suffer him, and that he would fight against him; wherefore he sought a way how to take Yahunatan, that he might kill him. So he removed, and came to Bethsan.

41 Then Yahunatan went out to meet him with forty thousand men chosen for the battle, and came to Bethsan.

42 Now when Tryphon saw Yahunatan came with so great a force, he durst not stretch his hand against him;

43 But received him honourably, and commended him unto all his friends, and gave him gifts, and commanded his men of war to be as obedient unto him, as to himself.

44 Unto Yahunatan also he said, Why have you brought all this people to so great trouble, seeing there is no war betwixt us?

45 Therefore send them now home again, and choose a few men to wait on you, and come you with me to Ptolemais, for I will give it you, and the rest of the strong holds and forces, and all that have any charge: as for me, I will return and depart: for this is the cause of my coming.

46 So Yahunatan believing him did as he bade him, and sent away his host, who went into the land of Y'hudah.

47 And with himself he retained but three thousand men, of whom he sent two thousand into Galil, and one thousand went with him.

48 Now as soon as Yahunatan entered into Ptolemais, they of Ptolemais shut the gates and took him, and all them that came with him they slew with the sword.

49 Then sent Tryphon an host of footmen and horsemen into Galil, and into the great plain, to destroy all Yahunatan's company.

50 But when they knew that Yahunatan and they that were with him were taken and slain, they encouraged one another; and went close together, prepared to fight.

51 They therefore that followed upon them, perceiving that they were ready to fight for their lives, turned back again.

52 Whereupon they all came into the land of Y'hudah peaceably, and there they bewailed Yahunatan, and them that were with him, and they were sore afraid; wherefore all Yisrael made great lamentation.

53 Then all the heathen that were round about then sought to destroy them: for said they, They have no captain, nor any to help them: now therefore let us make war upon them, and take away their memorial from among men.

CHAPTER 13

1 Now when Shim'on heard that Tryphon had gathered together a great host to invade the land of Y'hudah, and destroy it,

2 And saw that the people was in great trembling and fear, he went up to Yerushalayim, and gathered the people together,

3 And gave them exhortation, saying, Ye yourselves know what great things I, and my brothers, and my father's house, have done for the

laws and the sanctuary, the battles also and troubles which we have seen.

4 By reason whereof all my brothers are slain for Yisrael's sake, and I am left alone.

5 Now therefore be it far from me, that I should spare mine own life in any time of trouble: for I am no better than my brothers.

6 Doubtless I will avenge my nation, and the sanctuary, and our wives, and our children: for all the heathen are gathered to destroy us of very malice.

7 Now as soon as the people heard these words, their spirit revived.

8 And they answered with a loud voice, saying, You shall be our leader instead of Y'hudah and Yahunatan your brother.

9 Fight you our battles, and whatsoever, you command us, that will we do.

10 So then he gathered together all the men of war, and made haste to finish the walls of Yerushalayim, and he fortified it round about.

11 Also he sent Yahunatan the son of Absolom, and with him a great power, to Yafa: who casting out them that were therein remained there in it.

12 So Tryphon removed from Ptolemaus with a great power to invade the land of Y'hudah, and Yahunatan was with him in ward.

13 But Shim'on pitched his tents at Adida, over against the plain.

14 Now when Tryphon knew that Shim'on was risen up instead of his brother Yahunatan, and meant to join battle with him, he sent messengers unto him, saying,

15 Whereas we have Yahunatan your brother in hold, it is for money that he is owing unto the king's treasure, concerning the business that was committed unto him.

16 Wherefore now send an hundred talents of silver, and two of his sons for hostages, that when he is at liberty he may not revolt from us, and we will let him go.

17 Hereupon Shim'on, albeit he perceived that they spake deceitfully unto him yet sent he the money and the children, lest peradventure he should procure to himself great hatred of the people:

18 Who might have said, Because I sent him not the money and the children, therefore is Yahunatan dead.

19 So he sent them the children and the hundred talents: howbeit Tryphon dissembled neither would he let Yahunatan go.

20 And after this came Tryphon to invade the land, and destroy it, going round about by the way that leads unto Adora: but Shim'on and his host marched against him in every place, wheresoever he went.

21 Now they that were in the tower sent messengers unto Tryphon, to the end that he should hasten his coming unto them by the wilderness, and send them victuals.

22 Wherefore Tryphon made ready all his horsemen to come that night: but there fell a very great snow, by reason whereof he came not. So he departed, and came into the country of Gil'ad.

23 And when he came near to Bascama he slew Yahunatan, who was buried there.

24 Afterward Tryphon returned and went into his own land.

25 Then sent Shim'on, and took the bones of Yahunatan his brother, and buried them in Modin, the city of his fathers.

26 And all Yisrael made great lamentation for him, and bewailed him many days.

27 Shim'on also built a monument upon the sepulchre of his father and his brothers, and raised it aloft to the sight, with hewn stone behind and before.

28 Moreover he set up seven pyramids, one against another, for his father, and his mother, and his four brothers.

29 And in these he made cunning devices, about the which he set great pillars, and upon the pillars he made all their armour for a perpetual memory, and by the armour ships carved, that they might be seen of all that sail on the sea.

30 This is the sepulchre which he made at Modin, and it stands yet unto this day.

31 Now Tryphon dealt deceitfully with the young king Antiochus, and slew him.

32 And he reigned in his stead, and crowned himself king of Asia, and brought a great calamity upon the land.

33 Then Shim'on built up the strong holds in Y'hudah, and fenced them about with high towers, and great walls, and gates, and bars, and laid up victuals therein.

34 Moreover Shim'on chose men, and sent to king Demetrius, to the end he should give the land an immunity, because all that Tryphon did was to spoil.

35 Unto whom king Demetrius answered and wrote after this manner:

36 King Demetrius unto Shim'on the Cohen HaGadol, and friend of kings, as also unto the elders and nation of the Y'hudim, sends greeting:

37 The golden crown, and the scarlet robe, which you sent unto us, we have received: and we are ready to make a stedfast peace with you, yea, and to write unto our officers, to confirm the immunities which we have granted.

38 And whatsoever covenants we have made with you shall stand; and the strong holds, which you have built, shall be your own.

39 As for any oversight or fault committed unto this day, we forgive it, and the crown tax also, which you owe us: and if there were any other tribute paid in Yerushalayim, it shall no more be paid.

40 And look who are meet among you to be in our court, let then be enrolled, and let there be peace betwixt us.

41 Thus the yoke of the heathen was taken away from Yisrael in the hundred and seventieth year.

42 Then the people of Yisrael began to write in their instruments and contracts, In the first year of Shim'on the Cohen HaGadol, the governor and leader of the Y'hudim.

43 In those days Shim'on camped against Gaza and besieged it round about; he made also an engine of war, and set it by the city, and battered a certain tower, and took it.

44 And they that were in the engine leaped into the city; whereupon there was a great uproar in the city:

45 Insomuch as the people of the city rent their clothes, and climbed upon the walls with their wives and children, and cried with a loud voice, beseeching Shim'on to grant them peace.

46 And they said, Deal not with us according to our wickedness, but according to your mercy.

47 So Shim'on was appeased toward them, and fought no more against them, but put them out of the city, and cleansed the houses wherein the idols were, and so entered into it with songs and thanksgiving.

48 Yes, he put all uncleanness out of it, and placed such men there as would keep the Torah, and made it stronger than it was before, and built therein a dwellingplace for himself.

49 They also of the tower in Yerushalayim were kept so strait, that they could neither come forth, nor go into the country, nor buy, nor sell: wherefore they were in great distress for want of victuals, and a great number of them perished through famine.

50 Then cried they to Shim'on, beseeching him to be at one with them: which thing he granted them; and when he had put them out from thence, he cleansed the tower from pollutions:

51 And entered into it the three and twentieth day of the second month in the hundred seventy and first year, with thanksgiving, and branches of palm trees, and with harps, and cymbals, and with viols, and hymns, and songs: because there was destroyed a great enemy out of Yisrael.

52 He ordained also that that day should be kept every year with gladness. Moreover the hill of the Temple that was by the tower he

made stronger than it was, and there he dwelt himself with his company.

53 And when Shim'on saw that Yochanan his son was a valiant man, he made him captain of all the hosts; and he dwelt in Gazera.

CHAPTER 14

1 Now in the hundred threescore and twelfth year king Demetrius gathered his forces together, and went into Media to get him help to fight against Tryphone.

2 But when Arsaces, the king of Persia and Media, heard that Demetrius was entered within his borders, he sent one of his princes to take him alive:

3 Who went and smote the host of Demetrius, and took him, and brought him to Arsaces, by whom he was put in ward.

4 As for the land of Y'hudah, that was quiet all the days of Shim'on; for he sought the good of his nation in such wise, as that evermore his authority and honour pleased them well.

5 And as he was honourable in all his acts, so in this, that he took Yafa for an haven, and made an entrance to the isles of the sea,

6 And enlarged the bounds of his nation, and recovered the country,

7 And gathered together a great number of captives, and had the dominion of Gazera, and Beit-Tzur, and the tower, out of the which he took all uncleaness, neither was there any that resisted him.

8 Then did they till their ground in peace, and the earth gave her increase, and the trees of the field their fruit.

9 The ancient men sat all in the streets, communing together of good things, and the young men put on glorious and warlike apparel.

10 He provided victuals for the cities, and set in them all manner of munition, so that his honourable name was renowned unto the end of the world.

11 He made peace in the land, and Yisrael rejoiced with great joy:

12 For every man sat under his vine and his fig tree, and there was none to fray them:

13 Neither was there any left in the land to fight against them: yea, the kings themselves were overthrown in those days.

14 Moreover he strengthened all those of his people that were brought low: the Torah he searched out; and every contemner of the Torah and wicked person he took away.

15 He beautified the sanctuary, and multiplied vessels of the Temple.

16 Now when it was heard at Rome, and as far as Sparta, that Yahunatan was dead, they were very sorry.

17 But as soon as they heard that his brother Shim'on was made Cohen HaGadol in his stead, and ruled the country, and the cities therein:

18 They wrote unto him in tables of brass, to renew the friendship and league which they had made with Y'hudah and Yahunatan his brothers:

19 Which writings were read before the congregation at Yerushalayim.

20 And this is the copy of the letters that the Lacedemonians sent; The rulers of the Lacedemonians, with the city, unto Shim'on the Cohen HaGadol, and the elders, and cohenim, and residue of the people of the Y'hudim, our brothers, send greeting:

21 The ambassadors that were sent unto our people certified us of your glory and honour: wherefore we were glad of their coming,

22 And did register the things that they spake in the council of the people in this manner; Numenius son of Antiochus, and Antipater son of Jason, the Y'hudim' ambassadors, came unto us to renew the friendship they had with us.

23 And it pleased the people to entertain the men honourably, and to put the copy of their ambassage in publick records, to the end the people of the Lacedemonians might have a memorial thereof: furthermore we have written a copy thereof unto Shim'on the Cohen HaGadol.

24 After this Shim'on sent Numenius to Rome with a great shield of gold of a thousand pound weight to confirm the league with them.

25 Whereof when the people heard, they said, What thanks shall we give to Shim'on and his sons?

26 For he and his brothers and the house of his father have established Yisrael, and chased away in fight their enemies from them, and confirmed their liberty.

27 So then they wrote it in tables of brass, which they set upon pillars in mount Tzion: and this is the copy of the writing; The eighteenth day of the month Elul, in the hundred threescore and twelfth year, being the third year of Shim'on the Cohen HaGadol,

28 At Saramel in the great congregation of the cohenim, and people, and rulers of the nation, and elders of the country, were these things notified unto us.

29 Forasmuch as oftentimes there have been wars in the country, wherein for the maintenance of their sanctuary, and the Torah, Shim'on the son of Mattityahu, of the posterity of Jarib, together with

his brothers, put themselves in jeopardy, and resisting the enemies of their nation did their nation great honour:

30 (For after that Yahunatan, having gathered his nation together, and been their Cohen HaGadol, was added to his people,

31 Their enemies prepared to invade their country, that they might destroy it, and lay hands on the sanctuary:

32 At which time Shim'on rose up, and fought for his nation, and spent much of his own substance, and armed the valiant men of his nation and gave them wages,

33 And fortified the cities of Y'hudah, together with Beit-Tzur, that lies upon the borders of Y'hudah, where the armour of the enemies had been before; but he set a garrison of Y'hudim there:

34 Moreover he fortified Yafa, which lies upon the sea, and Gazera, that borders upon Azotus, where the enemies had dwelt before: but he placed Y'hudim there, and furnished them with all things convenient for the reparation thereof.)

35 The people therefore sang the acts of Shim'on, and unto what glory he thought to bring his nation, made him their governor and chief cohen, because he had done all these things, and for the justice and faith which he kept to his nation, and for that he sought by all means to exalt his people.

36 For in his time things prospered in his hands, so that the heathen were taken out of their country, and they also that were in the city of David in Yerushalayim, who had made themselves a tower, out of which they issued, and polluted all about the sanctuary, and did much hurt in the set-apart place:

37 But he placed Y'hudim therein. and fortified it for the safety of the country and the city, and raised up the walls of Yerushalayim.

38 King Demetrius also confirmed him in the Cohen HaGadolhood according to those things,

39 And made him one of his friends, and honoured him with great honour.

40 For he had heard say, that the Romans had called the Y'hudim their friends and confederates and brothers; and that they had entertained the ambassadors of Shim'on honourably;

41 Also that the Y'hudim and cohenim were well pleased that Shim'on should be their governor and Cohen HaGadol for ever, until there should arise a faithful prophet;

42 Moreover that he should be their captain, and should take charge of the sanctuary, to set them over their works, and over the country, and over the armour, and over the fortresses, that, I say, he should take charge of the sanctuary;

43 Beside this, that he should be obeyed of every man, and that all the writings in the country should be made in his name, and that he should be clothed in purple, and wear gold:

44 Also that it should be lawful for none of the people or cohenim to break any of these things, or to gainsay his words, or to gather an assembly in the country without him, or to be clothed in purple, or wear a buckle of gold;

45 And whosoever should do otherwise, or break any of these things, he should be punished.

46 Thus it liked all the people to deal with Shim'on, and to do as has been said.

47 Then Shim'on accepted hereof, and was well pleased to be Cohen HaGadol, and captain and governor of the Y'hudim and cohenim, and to defend them all.

48 So they commanded that this writing should be put in tables of brass, and that they should be set up within the compass of the sanctuary in a conspicuous place;

49 Also that the copies thereof should be laid up in the treasury, to the end that Shim'on and his sons might have them.

CHAPTER 15

1 Moreover Antiochus son of Demetrius the king sent letters from the isles of the sea unto Shim'on the cohen and prince of the Y'hudim, and to all the people;

2 The contents whereof were these: King Antiochus to Shim'on the Cohen HaGadol and prince of his nation, and to the people of the Y'hudim, greeting:

3 Forasmuch as certain pestilent men have usurped the kingdom of our fathers, and my purpose is to challenge it again, that I may restore it to the old estate, and to that end have gathered a multitude of foreign soldiers together, and prepared ships of war;

4 My meaning also being to go through the country, that I may be avenged of them that have destroyed it, and made many cities in the kingdom desolate:

5 Now therefore I confirm unto you all the oblations which the kings before me granted you, and whatsoever gifts besides they granted.

6 I give you leave also to coin money for your country with your own stamp.

7 And as concerning Yerushalayim and the sanctuary, let them be free; and all the armour that you have made, and fortresses that you have built, and keep in your hands, let them remain unto you.

8 And if anything be, or shall be, owing to the king, let it be forgiven you from this time forth for evermore.

9 Furthermore, when we have obtained our kingdom, we will honour you, and your nation, and your temple, with great honour, so that your honour shall be known throughout the world.

10 In the hundred threescore and fourteenth year went Antiochus into the land of his fathers: at which time all the forces came together unto him, so that few were left with Tryphon.

11 Wherefore being pursued by king Antiochus, he fled unto Dora, which lies by the sea side:

12 For he saw that troubles came upon him all at once, and that his forces had forsaken him.

13 Then camped Antiochus against Dora, having with him an hundred and twenty thousand men of war, and eight thousand horsemen.

14 And when he had compassed the city round about, and joined ships close to the town on the sea side, he vexed the city by land and by sea, neither suffered he any to go out or in.

15 In the mean season came Numenius and his company from Rome, having letters to the kings and countries; wherein were written these things:

16 Lucius, consul of the Romans unto king Ptolomy, greeting:

17 The Y'hudim' ambassadors, our friends and confederates, came unto us to renew the old friendship and league, being sent from Shim'on the Cohen HaGadol, and from the people of the Y'hudim:

18 And they brought a shield of gold of a thousand pound.

19 We thought it good therefore to write unto the kings and countries, that they should do them no harm, nor fight against them, their cities, or countries, nor yet aid their enemies against them.

20 It seemed also good to us to receive the shield of them.

21 If therefore there be any pestilent fellows, that have fled from their country unto you, deliver them unto Shim'on the Cohen HaGadol, that he may punish them according to their own law.

22 The same things wrote he likewise unto Demetrius the king, and Attalus, to Ariarathes, and Arsaces,

23 And to all the countries and to Sampsames, and the Lacedemonians, and to Delus, and Myndus, and Sicyon, and Caria, and Samos, and Pamphylia, and Lycia, and Halicarnassus, and Rhodus, and Aradus, and Cos, and Side, and Aradus, and Gortyna, and Cnidus, and Cyprus, and Cyrene.

24 And the copy hereof they wrote to Shim'on the Cohen HaGadol.
25 So Antiochus the king camped against Dora the second day, assaulting it continually, and making engines, by which means he shut up Tryphon, that he could neither go out nor in.
26 At that time Shim'on sent him two thousand chosen men to aid him; silver also, and gold, and much armour.
27 Nevertheless he would not receive them, but brake all the covenants which he had made with him afore, and became strange unto him.
28 Furthermore he sent unto him Athenobius, one of his friends, to commune with him, and say, Ye withhold Yafa and Gazera; with the tower that is in Yerushalayim, which are cities of my realm.
29 The borders thereof you have wasted, and done great hurt in the land, and got the dominion of many places within my kingdom.
30 Now therefore deliver the cities which you have taken, and the tributes of the places, whereof you have gotten dominion without the borders of Y'hudah:
31 Or else give me for them five hundred talents of silver; and for the harm that you have done, and the tributes of the cities, other five hundred talents: if not, we will come and fight against you
32 So Athenobius the king's friend came to Yerushalayim: and when he saw the glory of Shim'on, and the cupboard of gold and silver plate, and his great attendance, he was astonished, and told him the king's message.
33 Then answered Shim'on, and said unto him, We have neither taken other men's land, nor holden that which appertains to others, but the inheritance of our fathers, which our enemies had wrongfully in possession a certain time.
34 Wherefore we, having opportunity, hold the inheritance of our fathers.
35 And whereas you demand Yafa and Gazera, albeit they did great harm unto the people in our country, yet will we give you an hundred talents for them. Hereunto Athenobius answered him not a word;
36 But returned in a rage to the king, and made report unto him of these speeches, and of the glory of Shim'on, and of all that he had seen: whereupon the king was exceeding wroth.
37 In the mean time fled Tryphon by ship unto Orthosias.
38 Then the king made Cendebeus captain of the sea coast, and gave him an host of footmen and horsemen,
39 And commanded him to remove his host toward Y'hudah; also he commanded him to build up Cedron, and to fortify the gates, and to war against the people; but as for the king himself, he pursued Tryphon.

40 So Cendebeus came to Jamnia and began to provoke the people and to invade Y'hudah, and to take the people prisoners, and slay them.
41 And when he had built up Cedrou, he set horsemen there, and an host of footmen, to the end that issuing out they might make outroads upon the ways of Y'hudah, as the king had commanded him.

CHAPTER 16

1 Then came up Yochanan from Gazera, and told Shim'on his father what Cendebeus had done.
2 Wherefore Shim'on called his two eldest sons, Y'hudah and Yochanan, and said unto them, I, and my brothers, and my father's house, have ever from my youth unto this day fought against the enemies of Yisrael; and things have prospered so well in our hands, that we have delivered Yisrael oftentimes.
3 But now I am old, and you, by Elohim's mercy, are of a sufficient age: be you instead of me and my brother, and go and fight for our nation, and the help from heaven be with you.
4 So he chose out of the country twenty thousand men of war with horsemen, who went out against Cendebeus, and rested that night at Modin.
5 And when as they rose in the morning, and went into the plain, behold, a mighty great host both of footmen and horsemen came against them: howbeit there was a water brook betwixt them.
6 So he and his people pitched over against them: and when he saw that the people were afraid to go over the water brook, he went first over himself, and then the men seeing him passed through after him.
7 That done, he divided his men, and set the horsemen in the midst of the footmen: for the enemies' horsemen were very many.
8 Then sounded they with the set-apart trumpets: whereupon Cendebeus and his host were put to flight, so that many of them were slain, and the remnant gat them to the strong hold.
9 At that time was Y'hudah Yochanan's brother wounded; but Yochanan still followed after them, until he came to Cedron, which Cendebeus had built.
10 So they fled even unto the towers in the fields of Azotus; wherefore he burned it with fire: so that there were slain of them about two thousand men. Afterward he returned into the land of Y'hudah in peace.
11 Moreover in the plain of Yericho was Ptolemeus the son of Abubus made captain, and he had abundance of silver and gold:

12 For he was the Cohen HaGadol's son in law.

13 Wherefore his heart being lifted up, he thought to get the country to himself, and thereupon consulted deceitfully against Shim'on and his sons to destroy them.

14 Now Shim'on was visiting the cities that were in the country, and taking care for the good ordering of them; at which time he came down himself to Yericho with his sons, Mattityahu and Y'hudah, in the hundred threescore and seventeenth year, in the eleventh month, called Sabat:

15 Where the son of Abubus receiving them deceitfully into a little hold, called Docus, which he had built, made them a great banquet: howbeit he had hid men there.

16 So when Shim'on and his sons had drunk largely, Ptolomy and his men rose up, and took their weapons, and came upon Shim'on into the banqueting place, and slew him, and his two sons, and certain of his servants.

17 In which doing he committed a great treachery, and recompensed evil for good.

18 Then Ptolomy wrote these things, and sent to the king, that he should send him an host to aid him, and he would deliver him the country and cities.

19 He sent others also to Gazera to kill Yochanan: and unto the tribunes he sent letters to come unto him, that he might give them silver, and gold, and rewards.

20 And others he sent to take Yerushalayim, and the mountain of the Temple.

21 Now one had run afore to Gazera and told Yochanan that his father and brothers were slain, and that he, Ptolomy has sent to slay you also.

22 Hereof when he heard, he was sore astonished: so he laid hands on them that were come to destroy him, and slew them; for he knew that they sought to make him away.

23 As concerning the rest of the acts of Yochanan, and his wars, and worthy deeds which he did, and the building of the walls which he made, and his doings,

24 Behold, these are written in the chronicles of his priesthood, from the time he was made Cohen HaGadol after his father.

ספר מקבים ב
2Maccabim

CHAPTER 1

1 The brothers, the Y'hudim that be at Yerushalayim and in the land of Y'hudah, wish unto the brothers, the Y'hudim that are throughout Egypt, shalom, shalom and blessings be with you:

2 Elohim be good to you, and remember his covenant that he made with Avraham, Yiz'chak, and Ya'akov, his faithful servants;

3 And give you all an heart to serve him, and to do his will, with a good courage and a willing mind;

4 And open your hearts in his Torah and commandments, and send you shalom,

5 And hear your prayers, and be at one with you, and never forsake you in time of trouble.

6 And now we are here praying for you.

7 What time as Demetrius reigned, in the hundred threescore and ninth year, we the Y'hudim wrote unto you in the extremity of trouble that came upon us in those years, from the time that Jason and his company revolted from the set-apart land and kingdom,

8 And burned the porch, and shed innocent blood: then we prayed unto YHWH, and were heard; we offered also sacrifices and fine flour, and lit the menorahs, and set forth the loaves.

9 And now see that you keep the feast of Sukkot in the month Kislev.

10 In the hundred fourscore and eighth year, the people that were at Yerushalayim and in Y'hudah, and the council, and Y'hudah, sent greeting and health unto Aristobulus, king Ptolemeus' master, who was of the stock of the anointed cohenim, and to the Y'hudim that were in Egypt:

11 Insomuch as Elohim has delivered us from great perils, we thank him highly, as having been in battle against a king.

12 For he cast them out that fought within the set-apart city.

13 For when the leader was come into Persia, and the army with him that seemed invincible, they were slain in the Temple of Nanea by the deceit of Nanea's priests.

14 For Antiochus, as though he would marry her, came into the place, and his friends that were with him, to receive money in name of a dowry.

15 Which when the priests of Nanea had set forth, and he was entered with a small company into the compass of the Temple, they shut the Temple as soon as Antiochus was come in:

16 And opening a privy door of the roof, they threw stones like thunderbolts, and struck down the captain, hewed them in pieces, smote off their heads and cast them to those that were without.

17 Blessed be our Elohim in all things, who has delivered up the ungodly.

18 Therefore whereas we are now purposed to keep the purification of the Temple upon the five and twentieth day of the month Kislev, we thought it necessary to certify you thereof, that you also might keep it, like the feast of the Sukkot, and of the fire, which was given us when Nechemyah offered sacrifice, after that he had built the Temple and the altar.

19 For when our fathers were led into Persia, the cohenim that were then devout took the fire of the altar privily, and hid it in an hollow place of a pit without water, where they kept it sure, so that the place was unknown to all men.

20 Now after many years, when it pleased Elohim, Nechemyah, being sent from the king of Persia, did send of the posterity of those cohenim that had hid it to the fire: but when they told us they found no fire, but thick water;

21 Then commanded he them to draw it up, and to bring it; and when the sacrifices were laid on, Nechemyah commanded the cohenim to sprinkle the wood and the things laid thereupon with the water.

22 When this was done, and the time came that the sun shone, which afore was hid in the cloud, there was a great fire kindled, so that every man marvelled.

23 And the cohenim made a prayer whilst the sacrifice was consuming, I say, both the cohenim, and all the rest, Yahunatan beginning, and the rest answering thereunto, as Nechemyah did.

24 And the prayer was after this manner; O YHWH, YHWH Elohim, Creator of all things, who are fearful and strong, and righteous, and merciful, and the only and gracious King,

25 The only giver of all things, the only just, almighty, and everlasting, you that deliver Yisrael from all trouble, and did choose the fathers, and sanctify them:

26 Receive the sacrifice for your whole people Yisrael, and preserve your own portion, and sanctify it.

27 Gather those together that are scattered from us[42], deliver them that serve among the heathen, look upon them that are despised and abhorred, and let the heathen know that you are our Elohim.

28 Punish them that oppress us, and with pride do us wrong.

29 Plant your people again in your set-apart place, as Moshe has spoken[43].

30 And the cohenim sung psalms of thanksgiving.

31 Now when the sacrifice was consumed, Nechemyah commanded the water that was left to be poured on the great stones.

32 When this was done, there was kindled a flame: but it was consumed by the light that shined from the altar.

33 So when this matter was known, it was told the king of Persia, that in the place, where the cohenim that were led away had hid the fire, there appeared water, and that Nechemyah had purified the sacrifices therewith.

34 Then the king, inclosing the place, made it set-apart, after he had tried the matter.

35 And the king took many gifts, and bestowed thereof on those whom he would gratify.

36 And Nechemyah called this thing Naphthar, which is as much as to say, a cleansing: but many men call it Nephi.

CHAPTER 2

1 It is also found in the records, that Yeremiyahu the prophet commanded them that were carried away to take of the fire, as it has been signified:

2 And how that the prophet, having given them the Torah, charged them not to forget the commandments of YHWH, and that they should not err in their minds, when they see images of silver and gold, with their ornaments.

3 And with other such speeches exhorted he them, that the Torah should not depart from their hearts.

4 It was also contained in the same writing, that the prophet, being warned of Elohim, commanded the tabernacle and the ark to go with

---

[42] Deut. 30:3; Is. 11:12
[43] Deut. 30:5

him, as he went forth onto the mountain, where Moshe climbed up[44], and saw the heritage of YHWH[45].

5 And when Yeremiyahu came thither, he found an hollow cave, wherein he laid the tabernacle, and the ark, and the altar of incense, and so stopped the door.

6 And some of those that followed him came to mark the way, but they could not find it.

7 Which when Yeremiyahu perceived, he blamed them, saying, As for that place, it shall be unknown until the time that Elohim gather his people again together, and receive them unto mercy.

8 Then shall YHWH show them these things, and the glory of YHWH shall appear, and the cloud also, as it was showed under Moshe, and as when Shlomo desired that the place might be honourably sanctified.

9 It was also declared, that he being wise offered the sacrifice of dedication, and of the finishing of the Temple[46].

10 And as when Moshe prayed unto YHWH, the fire came down from heaven, and consumed the sacrifices[47]: even so prayed Shlomo also, and the fire came down from heaven, and consumed the burnt offerings[48].

11 And Moshe said, Because the sin offering was not to be eaten, it was consumed[49].

12 So Shlomo kept those eight days[50].

13 The same things also were reported in the writings and commentaries of Nechemyah; and how he founding a library gathered together the acts of the kings, and the prophets, and of David, and the epistles of the kings concerning the set-apart gifts.

14 In like manner also Y'hudah gathered together all those things that were lost by reason of the war we had, and they remain with us,

15 Wherefore if you have need thereof, send some to fetch them unto you.

16 Whereas we then are about to celebrate the purification, we have written unto you, and you shall do well, if you keep the same days.

17 We hope also, that the Elohim, that delivered all his people, and gave them all a heritage, and the kingdom, and the priesthood, and the sanctuary,

---

[44] i.e. Mount Nebo (Deut. 32:49)

[45] Aramaic: מריא "YHWH" Greek: Θεου "Elohim/Elohim"

[46] 1Kn. 3:2-28; 4:29-34; 8:62-64

[47] Lev. 9:24

[48] 2Chron. 7:1

[49] Lev. 10:16-19

[50] 1Kn. 8:65; 2Chron. 7:9

18 As he promised in the Torah, will shortly have mercy upon us, and gather us together out of every land under heaven into the set-apart place[51]: for he has delivered us out of great troubles, and has purified the place.

19 Now as concerning Y'hudah Maccabee, and his brothers, and the purification of the great Temple, and the dedication of the altar,

20 And the wars against Antiochus Epiphanes, and Eupator his son,

21 And the manifest signs that came from heaven unto those that behaved themselves manfully to their honour for Judaism[52]: so that, being but a few, they overcame the whole country, and chased barbarous multitudes,

22 And recovered again the Temple renowned all the world over, and freed the city, and upheld the laws which were going down, YHWH being gracious unto them with all favour:

23 All these things, I say, being declared by Jason of Cyrene in five books, we will assay to abridge in one volume.

24 For considering the infinite number, and the difficulty which they find that desire to look into the narrations of the story, for the variety of the matter,

25 We have been careful, that they that will read may have delight, and that they that are desirous to commit to memory might have ease, and that all into whose hands it comes might have profit.

26 Therefore to us, that have taken upon us this painful labour of abridging, it was not easy, but a matter of sweat and watching;

27 Even as it is no ease unto him that prepares a banquet, and seeks the benefit of others: yet for the pleasuring of many we will undertake gladly this great pain;

28 Leaving to the author the exact handling of every particular, and labouring to follow the rules of an abridgement.

29 For as the master builder of a new house must care for the whole building; but he that undertakes to set it out, and paint it, must seek out fit things for the adorning thereof: even so I think it is with us.

30 To stand upon every point, and go over things at large, and to be curious in particulars, belongs to the first author of the story:

31 But to use brevity, and avoid much labouring of the work, is to be granted to him that will make an abridgment.

32 Here then will we begin the story: only adding thus much to that which has been said, that it is a foolish thing to make a long prologue, and to be short in the story itself.

---

[51] Deut. 30:3, 5; Is. 11:12
[52] This is the first known usage of the term "Judaism"

CHAPTER 3

1 Now when the set-apart city was inhabited in shalom, and the laws were kept very well, because of the godliness of Onias the Cohen Ha-Gadol, and his hatred of wickedness,

2 It came to pass that even the kings themselves did honour the place, and magnify the Temple with their best gifts;

3 Insomuch that Seleucus of Asia of his own revenues bare all the costs belonging to the service of the sacrifices.

4 But one Shim'on of the tribe of Benjamin, who was made governor of the Temple, fell out with the Cohen Ha-Gadol about disorder in the city.

5 And when he could not overcome Onias, he gat him to Apollonius the son of Thraseas, who then was governor of Celosyria and Phenice,

6 And told him that the treasury in Yerushalayim was full of infinite sums of money, so that the multitude of their riches, which did not pertain to the account of the sacrifices, was innumerable, and that it was possible to bring all into the king's hand.

7 Now when Apollonius came to the king, and had showed him of the money whereof he was told, the king chose out Heliodorus his treasurer, and sent him with a commandment to bring him the foresaid money.

8 So forthwith Heliodorus took his journey; under a colour of visiting the cities of Celosyria and Phenice, but indeed to fulfil the king's purpose.

9 And when he was come to Yerushalayim, and had been courteously received of the Cohen Ha-Gadol of the city, he told him what intelligence was given of the money, and declared wherefore he came, and asked if these things were so indeed.

10 Then the Cohen Ha-Gadol told him that there was such money laid up for the relief of widows and fatherless children:

11 And that some of it belonged to Hircanus son of Toviyah, a man of great dignity, and not as that wicked Shim'on had misinformed: the sum whereof in all was four hundred talents of silver, and two hundred of gold:

12 And that it was altogether impossible that such wrongs should be done unto them, that had committed it to the holiness of the place, and to the majesty and inviolable sanctity of the Temple, honoured over all the world.

13 But Heliodorus, because of the king's commandment given him, said, That in any wise it must be brought into the king's treasury.

14 So at the day which he appointed he entered in to order this matter: wherefore there was no small agony throughout the whole city.

15 But the cohenim, prostrating themselves before the altar in their cohenim' vestments, called unto heaven upon him that made a Torah concerning things given to he kept, that they should safely be preserved for such as had committed them to be kept.

16 Then whoso had looked the Cohen Ha-Gadol in the face, it would have wounded his heart: for his countenance and the changing of his colour declared the inward agony of his mind.

17 For the man was so compassed with fear and horror of the body, that it was manifest to them that looked upon him, what sorrow he had now in his heart.

18 Others ran flocking out of their houses to the general supplication, because the place was like to come into contempt.

19 And the women, girt with sackcloth under their breasts, abounded in the streets, and the virgins that were kept in ran, some to the gates, and some to the walls, and others looked out of the windows.

20 And all, holding their hands toward heaven, made supplication.

21 Then it would have pitied a man to see the falling down of the multitude of all sorts, and the fear of the Cohen Ha-Gadol being in such an agony.

22 They then called upon the only Elohim[53] to keep the things committed of trust safe and sure for those that had committed them.

23 Nevertheless Heliodorus executed that which was decreed.

24 Now as he was there present himself with his guard about the treasury, YHWH of spirits[54], and the Elohim of all power and of all authoritiy[55],caused a great apparition, so that all that presumed to come in with him were astonished at the power of Elohim, and fainted, and were sore afraid.

25 For there appeared unto them an horse with a terrible rider upon him, and adorned with a very fair covering, and he ran fiercely, and

---

[53] "only Elohim" many translations have "Almighty Lord"; Aramaic: אלהא איחד "the only Elohim"; Greek: παντοκρατορα Θεον "All powerful Elohim".

[54] מריא דרוחתא This phrase "Lord of Spirits" also appears in the Ethiopic of the Book of Enoch in the Book of Parabales section where I have (in my translation of 1Enoch) taken it to represent **YHWH Tz'vaot** "YHWH of Hosts" in the lost original Hebrew of 1Enoch.

[55] "the Elohim of all power and of all authoritiy" Aramaic: אלהא דכלא חילא ודכלא שולטן The Greek text has "Prince of all power".

smote at Heliodorus with his forefeet, and it seemed that he that sat upon the horse had complete harness of gold.

26 Moreover two other young men appeared before him, notable in strength, excellent in beauty, and comely in apparel, who stood by him on either side; and scourged him continually, and gave him many sore stripes.

27 And Heliodorus fell suddenly unto the ground, and was compassed with great darkness: but they that were with him took him up, and put him into a litter.

28 Thus him, that lately came with a great train and with all his guard into the said treasury, they carried out, being unable to help himself with his weapons: and manifestly they acknowledged the power of Elohim.

29 For he by divine intervention was cast down, and lay speechless without all hope of life.

30 But they praised YHWH, that had miraculously honoured his own place: for the Temple; which a little afore was full of fear and trouble, when the only YHWH[56] appeared, was filled with joy and gladness.

31 Then straightways certain of Heliodorus' friends prayed Onias, that he would call upon the Most High to grant him his life, who lay ready to give up his last breath.

32 So the Cohen Ha-Gadol, suspecting lest the king should misconceive that some treachery had been done to Heliodorus by the Y'hudim, offered a sacrifice for the health of the man.

33 Now as the Cohen Ha-Gadol was making an atonement, the same young men in the same clothing appeared and stood beside Heliodorus, saying, Give Onias the Cohen Ha-Gadol great thanks, insomuch as for his sake YHWH has granted you life:

34 And seeing that you have been scourged from heaven, declare unto all men the mighty power of Elohim. And when they had spoken these words, they appeared no more.

35 So Heliodorus, after he had offered sacrifice unto Elohim[57], and made great vows unto him that had saved his life, and saluted Onias, returned with his host to the king.

36 Then testified he to all men the works of the great Elohim, which he had seen with his eyes.

37 And when the king Heliodorus, who might be a fit man to be sent yet once again to Yerushalayim, he said,

---

[56] "only YHWH" Aramaic: מריא איחד

[57] Aramaic: אלהא "Elohim/Elohim" Greek: Κυριω "Lord"

38 If you have any enemy or traitor, send him thither, and you shall receive him well scourged, if he escape with his life: for in that place, no doubt; there is an especial power of Elohim.

39 For he that dwells in heaven has his eye on that place, and defends it; and he beats and destroys them that come to hurt it.

40 And the things concerning Heliodorus, and the keeping of the treasury, fell out on this sort.

CHAPTER 4

1 This Shim'on now, of whom we spake afore, having been a betrayer of the money, and of his country, slandered Onias, as if he ha terrified Heliodorus, and been the worker of these evils.

2 Thus was he bold to call him a traitor, that had deserved well of the city, and tendered his own nation, and was so zealous of the laws.

3 But when their hatred went so far, that by one of Shim'on's faction murders were committed,

4 Onias seeing the danger of this contention, and that Apollonius, as being the governor of Celosyria and Phenice, did rage, and increase Shim'on's malice,

5 He went to the king, not to be an accuser of his countrymen, but seeking the good of all, both publick and private:

6 For he saw that it was impossible that the state should continue quiet, and Shim'on leave his folly, unless the king did look thereunto.

7 But after the death of Seleucus, when Antiochus, called Epiphanes, took the kingdom, Jason the brother of Onias laboured underhand to be Cohen Ha-Gadol,

8 Promising unto the king by intercession three hundred and threescore talents of silver, and of another revenue eighty talents:

9 Beside this, he promised to assign an hundred and fifty more, if he might have licence to set him up a place for exercise, and for the training up of youth in the fashions of the heathen, and to write them of Yerushalayim by the name of Antiochians.

10 Which when the king had granted, and he had gotten into his hand the rule he forthwith brought his own nation to Helenistic fashion.

11 And the royal privileges granted of special favour to the Y'hudim by the means of Yochanan the father of Eupolemus, who went ambassador to Rome for amity and aid, he took away; and putting down the governments which were according to the Torah, he brought up new customs against the Torah:

12 For he built gladly a place of exercise under the tower itself, and brought the chief young men under his subjection, and made them wear a hat.

13 Now such was the height of Greek fashions, and increase of heathenish manners, through the exceeding profaneness of Jason, that ungodly wretch, and no Cohen Ha-Gadol;

14 That the cohenim had no courage to serve any more at the altar, but despising the Temple, and neglecting the sacrifices, hastened to be partakers of the unlawful allowance in the place of exercise, after the game of Discus called them forth;

15 Not setting by the honours of their fathers, but liking the glory of the Greeks best of all.

16 By reason whereof sore calamity came upon them: for they had them to be their enemies and avengers, whose custom they followed so earnestly, and unto whom they desired to be like in all things.

17 For it is not a light thing to do wickedly against the set-apart Torah: but the time following shall declare these things.

18 Now when the games that were held every fourth year was kept at Tyrus, the king being present,

19 This ungracious Jason sent special messengers from Yerushalayim, who were Antiochians, to carry three hundred drachms of silver to the sacrifice of Hercules, which even the bearers thereof thought fit not to bestow upon the sacrifice, because it was not convenient, but to be reserved for other charges.

20 This money then, in regard of the sender, was appointed to Hercules' sacrifice; but because of the bearers thereof, it was employed to the making of gallies.

21 Now when Apollonius the son of Menestheus was sent into Egypt for the coronation of king Ptolemeus Philometor, Antiochus, understanding him not to be well affected to his affairs, provided for his own safety: whereupon he came to Yafa, and from thence to Yerushalayim:

22 Where he was honourably received of Jason, and of the city, and was brought in with torch alight, and with great shoutings: and so afterward went with his host unto Phenice.

23 Three years afterward Jason sent Menelans, the aforesaid Shim'on's brother, to bear the money unto the king, and to put him in mind of certain necessary matters.

24 But he being brought to the presence of the king, when he had magnified him for the glorious appearance of his power, got the priesthood to himself, offering more than Jason by three hundred talents of silver.

25 So he came with the king's mandate, bringing nothing worthy the Cohen HaGadolhood, but having the fury of a cruel tyrant, and the rage of a savage beast.

26 Then Jason, who had undermined his own brother, being undermined by another, was compelled to flee into the country of the Ammonites.

27 So Menelans got the principality: but as for the money that he had promised unto the king, he took no good order for it, albeit Sostratis the ruler of the citadel required it:

28 For unto him appertained the gathering of the customs. Wherefore they were both called before the king.

29 Now Menelans left his brother Lysimachus in his stead in the priesthood; and Sostratus left Crates, who was governor of the Cyprians.

30 While those things were in doing, they of Tarsus and Mallos made insurrection, because they were given to the king's concubine, called Antiochus.

31 Then came the king in all haste to appease matters, leaving Andronicus, a man in authority, for his deputy.

32 Now Menelans, supposing that he had gotten a convenient time, stole certain vessels of gold out of the Temple, and gave some of them to Andronicus, and some he sold into Tyrus and the cities round about.

33 Which when Onias knew of a surety, he reproved him, and withdrew himself into a sanctuary at Daphne, that lies by Antiochia.

34 Wherefore Menelans, taking Andronicus apart, prayed, him to get Onias into his hands; who being persuaded thereunto, and coming to Onias in deceit, gave him his right hand with oaths; and though he were suspected by him, yet persuaded he him to come forth of the sanctuary: whom forthwith he shut up without regard of justice.

35 For the which cause not only the Y'hudim, but many also of other nations, took great indignation, and were much grieved for the unjust murder of the man.

36 And when the king was come again from the places about Cilicia, the Y'hudim that were in the city, and certain of the Greeks that abhorred the fact also, complained because Onias was slain without cause.

37 Therefore Antiochus was heartily sorry, and moved to pity, and wept, because of the sober and modest behaviour of him that was dead.

38 And being kindled with anger, forthwith he took away Andronicus his purple, and rent off his clothes, and leading him through the whole city unto that very place, where he had committed impiety against

Onias, there slew he the cursed murderer. Thus YHWH rewarded him his punishment, as he had deserved.

39 Now when many sacrileges had been committed in the city by Lysimachus with the consent of Menelans, and the fruit thereof was spread abroad, the multitude gathered themselves together against Lysimachus, many vessels of gold being already carried away.

40 Whereupon the common people rising, and being filled with rage, Lysimachus armed about three thousand men, and began first to offer violence; one Auranus being the leader, a man far gone in years, and no less in folly.

41 They then seeing the attempt of Lysimachus, some of them caught stones, some clubs, others taking handfuls of dust, that was next at hand, cast them all together upon Lysimachus, and those that set upon them.

42 Thus many of them they wounded, and some they struck to the ground, and all of them they forced to flee: but as for the churchrobber himself, him they killed beside the treasury.

43 Of these matters therefore there was an accusation laid against Menelans.

44 Now when the king came to Tyrus, three men that were sent from the senate pleaded the cause before him:

45 But Menelans, being now convicted, promised Ptolomy the son of Dorymenes to give him much money, if he would pacify the king toward him.

46 Whereupon Ptolomy taking the king aside into a certain gallery, as it were to take the air, brought him to be of another mind:

47 Insomuch that he discharged Menelans from the accusations, who notwithstanding was cause of all the mischief: and those poor men, who, if they had told their cause, yea, before the Scythians, should have been judged innocent, them he condemned to death.

48 Thus they that followed the matter for the city, and for the people, and for the set-apart vessels, did soon suffer unjust punishment.

49 Wherefore even they of Tyrus, moved with hatred of that wicked deed, caused them to be honourably buried.

50 And so through the covetousness of them that were of power Menelans remained still in authority, increasing in malice, and being a great traitor to the citizens.

CHAPTER 5

1 About the same time Antiochus prepared his second voyage into Egypt:

2 And then it happened, that through all the city, for the space almost of forty days, there were seen horsemen running in the air, in cloth of gold, and armed with lances, like a band of soldiers,

3 And troops of horsemen in array, encountering and running one against another, with shaking of shields, and multitude of pikes, and drawing of swords, and casting of darts, and glittering of golden ornaments, and harness of all sorts.

4 Wherefore every man prayed that that apparition might turn to good.

5 Now when there was gone forth a false rumour, as though Antiochus had been dead, Jason took at the least a thousand men, and suddenly made an assault upon the city; and they that were upon the walls being put back, and the city at length taken, Menelans fled into the citadel:

6 But Jason slew his own citizens without mercy, not considering that to get the day of them of his own nation would be a most unhappy day for him; but thinking they had been his enemies, and not his countrymen, whom he conquered.

7 Howbeit for all this he obtained not the principality, but at the last received shame for the reward of his treason, and fled again into the country of the Ammonites.

8 In the end therefore he had an unhappy return, being accused before Aretas the king of the Arabians, fleeing from city to city, pursued of all men, hated as a forsaker of the laws, and being had in abomination as an open enemy of his country and countrymen, he was cast out into Egypt.

9 Thus he that had driven many out of their country perished in a strange land, retiring to the Lacedemonians, and thinking there to find succour by reason of his kindred:

10 And he that had cast out many unburied had none to mourn for him, nor any solemn funerals at all, nor sepulchre with his fathers.

11 Now when this that was done came to the king's ear, he thought that Y'hudah had revolted: whereupon removing out of Egypt in a furious mind, he took the city by force of arms,

12 And commanded his men of war not to spare such as they met, and to slay such as went up upon the houses.

13 Thus there was killing of young and old, making away of men, women, and children, slaying of virgins and infants.

14 And there were destroyed within the space of three whole days fourscore thousand, whereof forty thousand were slain in the conflict; and no fewer sold than slain.

15 Yet was he not content with this, but presumed to go into the most set-apart temple of all the world; Menelans, that traitor to the laws, and to his own country, being his guide:

16 And taking the set-apart vessels with polluted hands, and with profane hands pulling down the things that were dedicated by other kings to the augmentation and glory and honour of the place, he gave them away.

17 And so haughty was Antiochus in mind, that he considered not that YHWH was angry for a while for the sins of them that dwelt in the city, and therefore his eye was not upon the place.

18 For had they not been formerly wrapped in many sins, this man, as soon as he had come, had forthwith been scourged, and put back from his presumption, as Heliodorus was, whom Seleucus the king sent to view the treasury.

19 Nevertheless Elohim did not choose the people for the place's sake, but the place far the people's sake.

20 And therefore the place itself, that was partaker with them of the adversity that happened to the nation, did afterward communicate in the benefits sent from YHWH: and as it was forsaken in the wrath of the Elohim, so again was set up with all glory.

21 So when Antiochus had carried out of the Temple a thousand and eight hundred talents, he departed in all haste unto Antiochia, weening in his pride to make the land navigable, and the sea passable by foot: such was the haughtiness of his mind.

22 And he left governors to vex the nation: at Yerushalayim, Philip, for his country a Phrygian, and for manners more barbarous than he that set him there;

23 And at Garizim, Andronicus; and besides, Menelans, who worse than all the rest bare an heavy hand over the citizens, having a malicious mind against his countrymen the Y'hudim.

24 He sent also that detestable ringleader Apollonius with an army of two and twenty thousand, commanding him to slay all those that were in their best age, and to sell the women and the younger sort:

25 Who coming to Yerushalayim, and pretending peace, did forbear till the set-apart day of the sabbath, when taking the Y'hudim keeping set-apart day, he commanded his men to arm themselves.

26 And so he slew all them that were gone to the celebrating of the sabbath, and running through the city with weapons slew great multitudes.

27 But Y'hudah Maccabee with nine others, or thereabout, withdrew himself into the wilderness, and lived in the mountains after the manner of beasts[58], with his company, who fed on herbs continually, lest they should be partakers of the pollution.

CHAPTER 6

1 Not long after this the king sent an old man of Athens to compel the Y'hudim to depart from the laws of their fathers, and not to live after the laws of Elohim:

2 And to pollute also the Temple in Yerushalayim[59], and to call it the Temple of Zeus[60] Olympius; and that in Garizim, of Zeus[61] the Defender of strangers, as they did desire that dwelt in the place.

3 The coming in of this mischief was sore and grievous to the people:

4 For the Temple was filled with riot and revelling by the Goyim, who dallied with harlots, and had to do with women within the circuit of the set-apart places, and besides that brought in things that were not lawful.

5 The altar also was filled with profane things, which the Torah forbids.

6 Neither was it lawful for a man to keep sabbath days or ancient fasts, or to profess himself at all to be a Jew.

7 And in the day of the king's birth every month they were brought by bitter constraint to eat of the sacrifices; and when the fast of Bacchus was kept, the Y'hudim were compelled to go in procession to Bacchus, carrying ivy.

8 Moreover there went out a decree to the neighbour cities of the heathen, by the suggestion of Ptolomy, against the Y'hudim, that they should observe the same fashions, and be partakers of their sacrifices:

9 And whoso would not conform themselves to the manners of the Goyim should be put to death. Then might a man have seen the present misery.

10 For there were two women brought, who had circumcised their children; whom when they had openly led round about the city, the babes handing at their breasts, they cast them down headlong from the wall.

---

[58] Heb. 1137
[59] Dan. 9:27; 11:31; 12:11; 1Macc. 1:54; Mt. 24:15; Mk. 13:14
[60] Aramaic: בעלשמין   "Ba'al of the heavens" Greek: Διος
[61] Aramaic: בעלשמין   "Ba'al of the heavens" Greek: Διος

11 And others, that had run together into caves near by, to keep the sabbath day secretly, being discovered by Philip, were all burnt together, because they made a conscience to help themselves for the honour of the most sacred day.

12 Now I beseech those that read this book, that they be not discouraged for these calamities, but that they judge those punishments not to be for destruction, but for a chastening of our nation.

13 For it is a token of his great goodness, when wicked doers are not suffered any long time, but forthwith punished.

14 For not as with other nations, whom YHWH patiently forbears to punish, till they be come to the fulness of their sins, so deals he with us,

15 Lest that, being come to the height of sin, afterwards he should take vengeance of us.

16 And therefore he never withdraws his mercy from us: and though he punish with adversity, yet doth he never forsake his people.

17 But let this that we at spoken be for a warning unto us. And now will we come to the declaring of the matter in a few words.

18 El'azar, one of the principal scribes, an aged man, and of a well favoured countenance, was constrained to open his mouth, and to eat swine's flesh.

19 But he, choosing rather to die gloriously, than to live stained with such an abomination, spit it forth, and came of his own accord to the torment,

20 As it behoved them to come, that are resolute to stand out against such things, as are not lawful for love of life to be tasted.

21 But they that had the charge of that wicked feast, for the old acquaintance they had with the man, taking him aside, besought him to bring flesh of his own provision, such as was lawful for him to use, and make as if he did eat of the flesh taken from the sacrifice commanded by the king;

22 That in so doing he might be delivered from death, and for the old friendship with them find favour.

23 But he began to consider discreetly, and as became his age, and the excellency of his ancient years, and the honour of his gray head, whereon was come, and his most honest education from a child, or rather the set-apart Torah made and given by Elohim: therefore he answered accordingly, and willed them straightways to send him to the grave.

24 For it becomes not our age, said he, in any wise to dissemble, whereby many young persons might think that El'azar, being fourscore years old and ten, were now gone to a strange religion;

25 And so they through my hypocrisy, and desire to live a little time and a moment longer, should be deceived by me, and I get a stain to my old age, and make it abominable.

26 For though for the present time I should be delivered from the punishment of men: yet should I not escape the hand of Elohim, neither alive, nor dead.

27 Wherefore now, manfully changing this life, I will show myself such an one as my age requires,

28 And leave a notable example to such as be young to die willingly and courageously for the honourable and set-apart laws. And when he had said these words, immediately he went to the torment:

29 They that led him changing the good will they bare him a little before into hatred, because the foresaid speeches proceeded, as they thought, from a desperate mind.

30 But when he was ready to die with stripes, he groaned, and said, It is manifest unto YHWH, that has the set-apart knowledge, that whereas I might have been delivered from death, I now endure sore pains in body by being beaten: but in soul am well content to suffer these things, because I fear him.

31 And thus this man died, leaving his death for an example of a noble courage, and a memorial of virtue, not only unto young men, but unto all his nation.

CHAPTER 7

1 It came to pass also, that seven brothers with their mother were taken, and compelled by the king against the Torah to taste swine's flesh, and were tormented with scourges and whips.

2 But one of them that spake first said thus, What would you ask or learn of us? we are ready to die, rather than to transgress the laws of our fathers.

3 Then the king, being in a rage, commanded pans and caldrons to be made hot:

4 Which forthwith being heated, he commanded to cut out the tongue of him that spake first, and to cut off the utmost parts of his body, the rest of his brothers and his mother looking on.

5 Now when he was thus maimed in all his members, he commanded him being yet alive to be brought to the fire, and to be fried in the pan: and as the vapour of the pan was for a good space dispersed, they exhorted one another with the mother to die manfully, saying thus,

6 YHWH Elohim looks upon us, and in truth has comfort in us, as Moshe in his song, which witnessed to their faces, declared, saying, And he shall be comforted in his servants.

7 So when the first was dead after this number, they brought the second to make him a mocking stock: and when they had pulled off the skin of his head with the hair, they asked him, Will you eat, before you be punished throughout every member of your body?

8 But he answered in his own language, and said, No. Wherefore he also received the next torment in order, as the former did.

9 And when he was at the last gasp, he said, You like a fury take us out of this present life, but the King of the world shall raise us up, who have died for his laws, unto everlasting life.

10 After him was the third made a mocking stock: and when he was required, he put out his tongue, and that right soon, holding forth his hands manfully.

11 And said courageously, These I had from heaven; and for his laws I despise them; and from him I hope to receive them again.

12 Insomuch that the king, and they that were with him, marvelled at the young man's courage, for that he nothing regarded the pains.

13 Now when this man was dead also, they tormented and mangled the fourth in like manner.

14 So when he was ready to die he said thus, It is good, being put to death by men, to look for hope from Elohim to be raised up again by him: as for you, you shall have no resurrection to life.

15 Afterward they brought the fifth also, and mangled him.

16 Then looked he unto the king, and said, You have power over men, you are corruptible, you does what you will; yet think not that our nation is forsaken of Elohim;

17 But abide a while, and behold his great power, how he will torment you and your seed.

18 After him also they brought the sixth, who being ready to die said, Be not deceived without cause: for we suffer these things for ourselves, having sinned against our Elohim: therefore marvellous things are done unto us.

19 But think not you, that take in hand to strive against Elohim, that you shall escape unpunished.

20 But the mother was marvellous above all, and worthy of honourable memory: for when she saw her seven sons slain within the space of one day, she bare it with a good courage, because of the hope that she had in YHWH.

21 Yes, she exhorted every one of them in her own language, filled with courageous spirits; and stirring up her womanish thoughts with a manly stomach, she said unto them,

22 I cannot tell how you came into my womb: for I neither gave you breath nor life, neither was it I that formed the members of every one of you;

23 But doubtless the Creator of the world, who formed the generation of man, and found out the beginning of all things, will also of his own mercy give you breath and life again, as you now regard not your own selves for the sake of His Torah.

24 Now Antiochus, thinking himself despised, and suspecting it to be a reproachful speech, while the youngest was yet alive, did not only exhort him by words, but also assured him with oaths, that he would make him both a rich and a happy man, if he would turn from the laws of his fathers; and that also he would take him for his friend, and trust him with affairs.

25 But when the young man would in no case hearken unto him, the king called his mother, and exhorted her that she would counsel the young man to save his life.

26 And when he had exhorted her with many words, she promised him that she would counsel her son.

27 But she bowing herself toward him, laughing the cruel tyrant to scorn, spake in her country language on this manner; O my son, have pity upon me that bare you nine months in my womb, and gave you such three years, and nourished you, and brought you up unto this age, and endured the troubles of education.

28 I beseech you, my son, look upon the heaven and the earth, and all that is therein, and consider that Elohim made them of things that were not; and so was mankind made likewise[62].

29 Fear not this tormentor, but, being worthy of your brothers, take your death that I may receive you again in mercy with your brothers.

30 While she was yet speaking these words, the young man said, Whom wait you for? I will not obey the king's commandment: but I will obey the commandment of the Torah that was given unto our fathers by Moshe.

31 And you, that have been the author of all mischief against the Hebrews, shall not escape the hands of Elohim.

32 For we suffer because of our sins.

---

[62] The canonical scriptures lack such a clear statement that Elohim created the universe without any pre-existant material, but out of nothing.

33 And though YHWH our Elohim[63] be angry with us a little while for our chastening and correction, yet shall he be at one again with his servants.

34 But you, O godless man, and of all other most wicked, be not lifted up without a cause, nor puffed up with uncertain hopes, lifting up your hand against the servants of Elohim:

35 For you have not yet escaped the judgment of Almighty Elohim, who sees all things.

36 For our brothers, who now have suffered a short pain, are dead under Elohim's covenant of everlasting life: but you, through the judgment of Elohim, shall receive just punishment for your pride.

37 But I, as my brothers, offer up my body and life for the laws of our fathers, beseeching Elohim that he would speedily be merciful unto our nation; and that you by torments and plagues may confess, that he alone is Elohim;

38 And that in me and my brothers the wrath of the Almighty, which is justly brought upon our nation, may cease.

39 Than the king' being in a rage, handed him worse than all the rest, and took it grievously that he was mocked.

40 So this man died undefiled, and put his whole trust in YHWH.

41 Last of all after the sons the mother died.

42 Let this be enough now to have spoken concerning the idolatrous feasts, and the extreme tortures.

CHAPTER 8

1 Then Y'hudah Maccabee, and they that were with him, went privily into the towns, and called their kinsfolk together, and took unto them all such as continued in the Y'hudim' religion, and assembled about six thousand men.

2 And they called upon YHWH, that he would look upon the people that was trodden down of all; and also pity the Temple profaned of ungodly men;

3 And that he would have compassion upon the city, sore defaced, and ready to be made even with the ground; and hear the blood that cried unto him,

4 And remember the wicked slaughter of harmless infants, and the blasphemies committed against His Name; and that he would show his hatred against the wicked.

---

[63] Aramaic: מריא אלהן **אלהן** "YHWH our Elohim"; Greek: ζων Κυριος "Living Lord"

5 Now when Maccabee had his company about him, he could not be withstood by the heathen: for the wrath of Elohim[64] was turned into mercy.

6 Therefore he came at unawares, and burnt up towns and cities, and got into his hands the most commodious places, and overcame and put to flight no small number of his enemies.

7 But specially took he advantage of the night for such privy attempts, insomuch that the fruit of his holiness was spread every where.

8 So when Philip saw that this man increased by little and little, and that things prospered with him still more and more, he wrote unto Ptolemeus, the governor of Celosyria and Phenice, to yield more aid to the king's affairs.

9 Then forthwith choosing Nicanor the son of Patroclus, one of his special friends, he sent him with no fewer than twenty thousand of all nations under him, to root out the whole generation of the Y'hudim; and with him he joined also Gorgias a captain, who in matters of war had great experience.

10 So Nicanor undertook to make so much money of the captive Y'hudim, as should defray the tribute of two thousand talents, which the king was to pay to the Romans.

11 Wherefore immediately he sent to the cities upon the sea coast, proclaiming a sale of the captive Y'hudim, and promising that they should have fourscore and ten bodies for one talent, not expecting the vengeance that was to follow upon him from the only Elohim.

12 Now when word was brought unto Y'hudah of Nicanor's coming, and he had imparted unto those that were with him that the army was at hand,

13 They that were fearful, and distrusted the justice of Elohim, fled, and conveyed themselves away.

14 Others sold all that they had left, and withal besought from YHWH to deliver them, sold by the wicked Nicanor before they met together:

15 And if not for their own sakes, yet for the covenants he had made with their fathers, and for his set-apart and glorious name's sake, by which they were called.

16 So Maccabee called his men together unto the number of six thousand, and exhorted them not to be stricken with terror of the enemy, nor to fear the great multitude of the heathen, who came wrongly against them; but to fight manfully,

17 And to set before their eyes the injury that they had unjustly done to the set-apart place, and the cruel handling of the city, whereof they

---

[64] Aramaic: אלהא "Elohim; Elohim" Greek: Κυριου "Lord"

made a mockery, and also the taking away of the government of their forefathers:

18 For they, said he, trust in their weapons and boldness; but our confidence is in YHWH our only Elohim who at a beck can cast down both them that come against us, and also all the world.

19 Moreover, he recounted unto them what helps their forefathers had found, and how they were delivered, when under Sennacherib an hundred fourscore and five thousand perished[65].

20 And he told them of the battle that they had in Babylon with the Galatians, how they came but eight thousand in all to the business, with four thousand Macedonians, and that the Macedonians being perplexed, the eight thousand destroyed an hundred and twenty thousand because of the help that they had from heaven, and so received a great booty.

21 Thus when he had made them bold with these words, and ready to die for the Torah and the country, he divided his army into four parts;

22 And joined with himself his own brothers, leaders of each band, to wit Shim'on, and Yosef, and Yahunatan, giving each one fifteen hundred men.

23 Also he appointed El'azar to read the set-apart book: and when he had given them this watchword, The help of Elohim; himself leading the first band,

24 And by the help of the only Elohim they slew above nine thousand of their enemies, and wounded and maimed the most part of Nicanor's host, and so put all to flight;

25 And took their money that came to buy them, and pursued them far: but lacking time they returned:

26 For it was the day before the sabbath, and therefore they would no longer pursue them.

27 So when they had gathered their armour together, and spoiled their enemies, they occupied themselves about the sabbath, yielding exceeding praise and thanks to YHWH, who had preserved them unto that day, which was the beginning of mercy distilling upon them.

28 And after the sabbath, when they had given part of the spoils to the maimed, and the widows, and orphans, the residue they divided among themselves and their servants.

29 When this was done, and they had made a common supplication, they besought the merciful YHWH to be reconciled with his servants for ever.

---

[65] 2Kn. 19:35

30 Moreover of those that were with Timotheus and Bacchides, who fought against them, they slew above twenty thousand, and very easily got high and strong holds, and divided among themselves many spoils more, and made the maimed, orphans, widows, yea, and the aged also, equal in spoils with themselves.

31 And when they had gathered their armour together, they laid them up all carefully in convenient places, and the remnant of the spoils they brought to Yerushalayim.

32 They slew also Philarches, that wicked person, who was with Timotheus, and had annoyed the Y'hudim many ways.

33 Furthermore at such time as they kept the feast for the victory in their country they burnt Callisthenes, that had set fire upon the set-apart gates, who had fled into a little house; and so he received a reward meet for his wickedness.

34 As for that most ungracious Nicanor, who had brought a thousand merchants to buy the Y'hudim,

35 He was through the help of Elohim[66] brought down by them, of whom he made least account; and putting off his glorious apparel, and discharging his company, he came like a fugitive servant through the midland unto Antioch having very great dishonour, for that his host was destroyed.

36 Thus he, that took upon him to make good to the Romans their tribute by means of captives in Yerushalayim, told abroad, that the Y'hudim had Elohim to fight for them, and therefore they could not be hurt, because they followed the laws that he gave them.

CHAPTER 9

1 About that time came Antiochus with dishonour out of the country of Persia

2 For he had entered the city called Persepolis, and went about to rob the Temple, and to hold the city; whereupon the multitude running to defend themselves with their weapons put them to flight; and so it happened, that Antiochus being put to flight of the inhabitants returned with shame.

3 Now when he came to Ecbatane, news was brought him what had happened unto Nicanor and Timotheus.

4 Then swelling with anger. he thought to avenge upon the Y'hudim the disgrace done unto him by those that made him flee. Therefore

---

[66] Aramaic: אלהא "Elohim;Elohim" Greek: Κυριου "Lord"

commanded he his chariotman to drive without ceasing, and to dispatch the journey, the judgment of Elohim now following him. For he had spoken proudly in this sort, That he would come to Yerushalayim and make it a common burying place of the Y'hudim.

5 But YHWH the Elohim of Isreal, smote him with an incurable and invisible plague: or as soon as he had spoken these words, a pain of the bowels that was remediless came upon him, and sore torments of the inner parts;

6 And that most justly: for he had tormented other men's bowels with many and strange torments.

7 Howbeit he nothing at all ceased from his bragging, but still was filled with pride, breathing out fire in his rage against the Y'hudim, and commanding to haste the journey: but it came to pass that he fell down from his chariot, carried violently; so that having a sore fall, all the members of his body were much pained.

8 And thus he that a little afore thought he might command the waves of the sea, (so proud was he beyond the condition of man) and weigh the high mountains in a balance, was now cast on the ground, and carried in an horselitter, shewing forth unto all the manifest power of Elohim.

9 So that the worms rose up out of the body of this wicked man, and whiles he lived in sorrow and pain, his flesh fell away, and the filthiness of his smell was noisome to all his army.

10 And the man, that thought a little afore he could reach to the stars of heaven, no man could endure to carry for his intolerable stink.

11 Here therefore, being plagued, he began to leave off his great pride, and to come to the knowledge of himself by the scourge of Elohim, his pain increasing every moment.

12 And when he himself could not abide his own smell, he said these words, It is meet to be subject unto Elohim, and that a man that is mortal should not proudly think of himself if he were Elohim.

13 This wicked person vowed also unto YHWH, who now no more would have mercy upon him, saying thus,

14 That the set-apart city (to the which he was going in haste to lay it even with the ground, and to make it a common buryingplace,) he would set at liberty:

15 And as touching the Y'hudim, whom he had judged not worthy so much as to be buried, but to be cast out with their children to be devoured of the fowls and wild beasts, he would make them all equals to the citizens of Athens:

16 And the set-apart temple, which before he had spoiled, he would garnish with goodly gifts, and restore all the set-apart vessels with

many more, and out of his own revenue defray the charges belonging to the sacrifices:

17 Yes, and that also he would become a Jew himself, and go through all the world that was inhabited, and declare the power of Elohim.

18 But for all this his pains would not cease: for the just judgment of Elohim was come upon him: therefore despairing of his health, he wrote unto the Y'hudim the letter underwritten, containing the form of a supplication, after this manner:

19 Antiochus, king and governor, to the good Y'hudim his citizens wishes much joy, health, and prosperity:

20 If you and your children fare well, and your affairs be to your contentment, I give very great thanks to Elohim that is in heaven.

21 As for me, I was weak, or else I would have remembered kindly your honour and good will returning out of Persia, and being taken with a grievous disease, I thought it necessary to care for the common safety of all:

22 Not distrusting mine health, but having great hope to escape this sickness.

23 But considering that even my father, at what time he led an army into the high countries. appointed a successor,

24 To the end that, if any thing fell out contrary to expectation, or if any tidings were brought that were grievous, they of the land, knowing to whom the state was left, might not be troubled:

25 Again, considering how that the princes that are borderers and neighbours unto my kingdom wait for opportunities, and expect what shall be the event. I have appointed my son Antiochus king, whom I often committed and commended unto many of you, when I went up into the high provinces; to whom I have written as follows:

26 Therefore I pray and request you to remember the benefits that I have done unto you generally, and in special, and that every man will be still faithful to me and my son.

27 For I am persuaded that he understanding my mind will favourably and graciously yield to your desires.

28 Thus the murderer and blasphemer having suffered most grievously, as he entreated other men, so died he a miserable death in a strange country in the mountains.

29 And Philip, that was brought up with him, carried away his body, who also fearing the son of Antiochus went into Egypt to Ptolemeus Philometor.

CHAPTER 10

1 Now Maccabee and his company, YHWH guiding them, recovered the Temple and the city:

2 But the altars which the heathen had built in the open street, and also the chapels, they pulled down.

3 And having cleansed the Temple they made another altar, and striking stones they took fire out of them, and offered a sacrifice after two years, and set forth incense, and lights, and shewbread.

4 When that was done, they fell flat down, and besought YHWH that they might come no more into such troubles; but if they sinned any more against him, that he himself would chasten them with mercy, and that they might not be delivered unto the blasphemous and barbarous nations.

5 Now upon the same day that the strangers profaned the Temple, on the very same day it was cleansed again, even the five and twentieth day of the same month, which is Kislev.

6 And they kept the eight days with gladness, as in the feast of the Sukkot, remembering that not long afore they had held the feast of the Sukkot, when as they wandered in the mountains and dens like beasts.

7 Therefore they bare branches, and fair boughs, and palms also, and sang psalms unto him that had given them good success in cleansing his place.

8 They ordained also by a common statute and decree, That every year those days should be kept of the whole nation of the Y'hudim.

9 And this was the end of Antiochus, called Epiphanes.

10 Now will we declare the acts of Antiochus Eupator, who was the son of this wicked man, gathering briefly the calamities of the wars.

11 So when he was come to the crown, he set one Lysias over the affairs of his realm, and appointed him his chief governor of Celosyria and Phenice.

12 For Ptolemeus, that was called Macron, choosing rather to do justice unto the Y'hudim for the wrong that had been done unto them, endeavoured to continue peace with them.

13 Whereupon being accused of the king's friends before Eupator, and called traitor at every word because he had left Cyprus, that Philometor had committed unto him, and departed to Antiochus Epiphanes, and seeing that he was in no honourable place, he was so discouraged, that he poisoned himself and died.

14 But when Gorgias was governor of the holds, he hired soldiers, and nourished war continually with the Y'hudim:

15 And therewithall the Idumeans, having gotten into their hands the most commodious holds, kept the Y'hudim occupied, and receiving those that were banished from Yerushalayim, they went about to nourish war.

16 Then they that were with Maccabee made supplication, and besought Elohim that he would be their helper; and so they ran with violence upon the strong holds of the Idumeans,

17 And assaulting them strongly, they won the holds, and kept off all that fought upon the wall, and slew all that fell into their hands, and killed no fewer than twenty thousand.

18 And because certain, who were no less than nine thousand, were fled together into two very strong castles, having all manner of things convenient to sustain the siege,

19 Maccabee left Shim'on and Yosef, and Z'kharyah also, and them that were with him, who were enough to besiege them, and departed himself unto those places which more needed his help.

20 Now they that were with Shim'on, being led with covetousness, were persuaded for money through certain of those that were in the citadel, and took seventy thousand drachms, and let some of them escape.

21 But when it was told Maccabee what was done, he called the governors of the people together, and accused those men, that they had sold their brothers for money, and set their enemies free to fight against them.

22 So he slew those that were found traitors, and immediately took the two castles.

23 And having good success with his weapons in all things he took in hand, he slew in the two holds more than twenty thousand.

24 Now Timotheus, whom the Y'hudim had overcome before, when he had gathered a great multitude of foreign forces, and horses out of Asia not a few, came as though he would take Jewry by force of arms.

25 But when he drew near, they that were with Maccabee turned themselves to pray unto Elohim, and sprinkled earth upon their heads, and girded their loins with sackcloth,

26 And fell down at the foot of the altar, and besought him to be merciful to them, and to be an enemy to their enemies, and an adversary to their adversaries, as the Torah declares.

27 So after the prayer they took their weapons, and went on further from the city: and when they drew near to their enemies, they kept by themselves.

28 Now the sun being newly risen, they joined both together; the one part having together with their virtue their refuge also unto YHWH for

a pledge of their success and victory: the other side making their rage leader of their battle

29 But when the battle waxed strong, there appeared unto the enemies from heaven five comely men upon horses, with bridles of gold, and two of them led the Y'hudim,

30 And took Maccabee beween them, and covered him on every side weapons, and kept him safe, but shot arrows and lightnings against the enemies: so that being confounded with blindness, and full of trouble, they were killed.

31 And there were slain of footmen twenty thousand and five hundred, and six hundred horsemen.

32 As for Timotheus himself, he fled into a very strong hold, called Gawra, where Chereas was governor.

33 But they that were with Maccabee laid siege against the fortress courageously four days.

34 And they that were within, trusting to the strength of the place, blasphemed exceedingly, and uttered wicked words.

35 Nevertheless upon the fifth day early twenty young men of Maccabee' company, inflamed with anger because of the blasphemies, assaulted the wall manly, and with a fierce courage killed all that they met withal.

36 Others likewise ascending after them, whiles they were busied with them that were within, burnt the towers, and kindling fires burnt the blasphemers alive; and others broke open the gates, and, having received in the rest of the army, took the city,

37 And killed Timotheus, that was hid in a certain pit, and Chereas his brother, with Apollophanes.

38 When this was done, they praised Elohim[67] with psalms and thanksgiving, who had done so great things for Yisrael, and given them the victory.

CHAPTER 11

1 Not long after the, Lysias the king's protector and cousin, who also managed the affairs, took sore displeasure for the things that were done.

2 And when he had gathered about fourscore thousand with all the horsemen, he came against the Y'hudim, thinking to make the city an habitation of the Goyim,

---

[67] Aramaic: אלהא "Elohim;Elohim" Greek: Κυριου "Lord"

3 And to make a gain of the Temple, as of the other chapels of the heathen, and to set the Cohen HaGadolhood to sale every year:

4 Not at all considering the power of Elohim but puffed up with his ten thousands of footmen, and his thousands of horsemen, and his fourscore elephants.

5 So he came to Y'hudah, and drew near to Beit-Tzur, which was a strong town, but distant from Yerushalayim about five furlongs, and he laid sore siege unto it.

6 Now when they that were with Maccabee heard that he besieged the holds, they and all the people with lamentation and tears besought YHWH that he would send a good angel to deliver Yisrael.

7 Then Maccabee himself first of all took weapons, exhorting the other that they would jeopard themselves together with him to help their brothers: so they went forth together with a willing mind.

8 And as they were at Yerushalayim, there appeared before them on horseback one in white clothing, shaking his armour of gold.

9 Then they praised the merciful Elohim all together, and took heart, insomuch that they were ready not only to fight with men, but with most cruel beasts, and to pierce through walls of iron.

10 Thus they marched forward in their armour, having an helper from heaven: for Elohim[68] was merciful unto them

11 And giving a charge upon their enemies like lions, they slew eleven thousand footmen, and sixteen hundred horsemen, and put all the other to flight.

12 Many of them also being wounded escaped naked; and Lysias himself fled away shamefully, and so escaped.

13 Who, as he was a man of understanding, casting with himself what loss he had had, and considering that the Hebrews could not be overcome, because Elohim helped them, he sent unto them,

14 And persuaded them to agree to all reasonable conditions, and promised that he would persuade the king that he must needs be a friend unto them.

15 Then Maccabee consented to all that Lysias desired, being careful of the common good; and whatsoever Maccabee wrote unto Lysias concerning the Y'hudim, the king granted it.

16 For there were letters written unto the Y'hudim from Lysias to this effect: Lysias unto the people of the Y'hudim sends greeting:

17 Yochanan and Avshalom, who were sent from you, delivered me the petition subscribed, and made request for the performance of the contents thereof.

---

[68] Aramaic: אלהא "Elohim;Elohim" Greek: Κυριου "Lord"

18 Therefore what things soever were meet to be reported to the king, I have declared them, and he has granted as much as might be.

19 And if then you will keep yourselves loyal to the state, hereafter also will I endeavour to be a means of your good.

20 But of the particulars I have given order both to these and the other that came from me, to commune with you.

21 Fare you well. The hundred and eight and fortieth year, the four and twentieth day of the month Dioscorinthius.

22 Now the king's letter contained these words: King Antiochus unto his brother Lysias sends greeting:

23 Since our father is translated unto the gods, our will is, that they that are in our realm live quietly, that every one may attend upon his own affairs.

24 We understand also that the Y'hudim would not consent to our father, for to be brought unto the custom of the Goyim, but had rather keep their own manner of living: for the which cause they require of us, that we should suffer them to live after their own laws.

25 Wherefore our mind is, that this nation shall be in rest, and we have determined to restore them their temple, that they may live according to the customs of their forefathers.

26 You shall do well therefore to send unto them, and grant them peace, that when they are certified of our mind, they may be of good comfort, and ever go cheerfully about their own affairs.

27 And the letter of the king unto the nation of the Y'hudim was after this manner: King Antiochus sends greeting unto the council, and the rest of the Y'hudim:

28 If you fare well, we have our desire; we are also in good health.

29 Menelans declared unto us, that your desire was to return home, and to follow your own business:

30 Wherefore they that will depart shall have safe conduct till the thirtieth day of Xanthicus with security.

31 And the Y'hudim shall use their own kind of meats and laws, as before; and none of them any manner of ways shall be molested for things ignorantly done.

32 I have sent also Menelans, that he may comfort you.

33 Fare you well. In the hundred forty and eighth year, and the fifteenth day of the month Xanthicus.

34 The Romans also sent unto them a letter containing these words: Quintus Memmius and Titus Manlius, ambassadors of the Romans, send greeting unto the people of the Y'hudim.

35 Whatsoever Lysias the king's cousin has granted, therewith we also are well pleased.

36 But touching such things as he judged to be referred to the king, after you have advised thereof, send one forthwith, that we may declare as it is convenient for you: for we are now going to Antioch.

37 Therefore send some with speed, that we may know what is your mind.

38 Farewell. This hundred and eight and fortieth year, the fifteenth day of the month Xanthicus.

CHAPTER 12

1 When these covenants were made, Lysias went unto the king, and the Y'hudim were about their husbandry.

2 But of the governours of several places, Timotheus, and Apollonius the son of Genneus, also Hieronymus, and Demophon, and beside them Nicanor the governor of Cyprus, would not suffer them to be quiet and live in peace.

3 The men of Yafa also did such an ungodly deed: they prayed the Y'hudim that dwelt among them to go with their wives and children into the boats which they had prepared, as though they had meant them no hurt.

4 Who accepted of it according to the common decree of the city, as being desirous to live in peace, and suspecting nothing: but when they were gone forth into the deep, they drowned no less than two hundred of them.

5 When Y'hudah heard of this cruelty done unto his countrymen, he commanded those that were with him to make them ready.

6 And calling upon Elohim the righteous Judge, he came against those murderers of his brothers, and burnt the haven by night, and set the boats on fire, and those that fled thither he slew.

7 And when the town was shut up, he went backward, as if he would return to root out all them of the city of Yafa.

8 But when he heard that the Jamnites were minded to do in like manner unto the Y'hudim that dwelt among them,

9 He came upon the Jamnites also by night, and set fire on the haven and the navy, so that the light of the fire was seen at Yerushalayim two hundred and forty furlongs off.

10 Now when they were gone from thence nine furlongs in their journey toward Timotheus, no fewer than five thousand men on foot and five hundred horsemen of the Arabians set upon him.

11 Whereupon there was a very sore battle; but Y'hudah' side by the help of Elohim got the victory; so that the Nomades of Arabia, being

overcome, besought Y'hudah for peace, promising both to give him cattle, and to pleasure him otherwise.

12 Then Y'hudah, thinking indeed that they would be profitable in many things, granted them peace: whereupon they shook hands, and so they departed to their tents.

13 He went also about to make a bridge to a certain strong city, which was fenced about with walls, and inhabited by people of divers countries; and the name of it was Caspis.

14 But they that were within it put such trust in the strength of the walls and provision of victuals, that they behaved themselves rudely toward them that were with Y'hudah, railing and blaspheming, and uttering such words as were not to be spoken.

15 Wherefore Y'hudah with his company, calling upon the great YHWH of the world, who without rams or engines of war did cast down Yericho in the time of Joshua, gave a fierce assault against the walls,

16 And took the city by the will of Elohim, and made unspeakable slaughters, insomuch that a lake two furlongs broad near adjoining thereunto, being filled full, was seen running with blood.

17 Then departed they from thence seven hundred and fifty furlongs, and came to Characa unto the Y'hudim that are called Tubieni.

18 But as for Timotheus, they found him not in the places: for before he had dispatched any thing, he departed from thence, having left a very strong garrison in a certain hold.

19 Howbeit Dositheus and Sosipater, who were of Maccabee' captains, went forth, and slew those that Timotheus had left in the fortress, above ten thousand men.

20 And Maccabee ranged his army by bands, and set them over the bands, and went against Timotheus, who had about him an hundred and twenty thousand men of foot, and two thousand and five hundred horsemen.

21 Now when Timotheus had knowledge of Y'hudah' coming, he sent the women and children and the other baggage unto a fortress called Carnion: for the town was hard to besiege, and uneasy to come unto, by reason of the straitness of all the places.

22 But when Y'hudah his first band came in sight, the enemies, being smitten with fear and terror through the appearing of him who sees all things, fled amain, one running into this way, another that way, so as that they were often hurt of their own men, and wounded with the points of their own swords.

23 Y'hudah also was very earnest in pursuing them, killing those wicked wretches, of whom he slew about thirty thousand men.

24 Moreover Timotheus himself fell into the hands of Dositheus and Sosipater, whom he besought with much craft to let him go with his life, because he had many of the Y'hudim' parents, and the brothers of some of them, who, if they put him to death, should not be regarded.

25 So when he had assured them with many words that he would restore them without hurt, according to the agreement, they let him go for the saving of their brothers.

26 Then Maccabee marched forth to Carnion, and to the Temple of Atargatis, and there he slew five and twenty thousand persons.

27 And after he had put to flight and destroyed them, Y'hudah removed the host toward Ephron, a strong city, wherein Lysias abode, and a great multitude of divers nations, and the strong young men kept the walls, and defended them mightily: wherein also was great provision of engines and darts.

28 But when Y'hudah and his company had called upon Almighty Elohim, who with his power breaks the strength of his enemies, they won the city, and slew twenty and five thousand of them that were within,

29 From thence they departed to Scythopolis, which lies six hundred furlongs from Yerushalayim,

30 But when the Y'hudim that dwelt there had testified that the Scythopolitans dealt lovingly with them, and entreated them kindly in the time of their adversity;

31 They gave them thanks, desiring them to be friendly still unto them: and so they came to Yerushalayim, the feast of the weeks approaching.

32 And after the feast, called Pentecost[69], they went forth against Gorgias the governor of Idumea,

33 Who came out with three thousand men of foot and four hundred horsemen.

34 And it happened that in their fighting together a few of the Y'hudim were slain.

35 At which time Dositheus, one of Bacenor's company, who was on horseback, and a strong man, was still upon Gorgias, and taking hold of his coat drew him by force; and when he would have taken that cursed man alive, a horseman of Thracia coming upon him smote off his shoulder, so that Gorgias fled unto Marisa.

36 Now when they that were with Gorgias had fought long, and were weary, Y'hudah called upon YHWH, that he would show himself to be their helper and leader of the battle.

---

[69] or "Pentecost"

37 And with that he began in his own language, and sung psalms with a loud voice, and rushing unawares upon Gorgias' men, he put them to flight.

38 So Y'hudah gathered his host, and came into the city of Odollam, And when the seventh day came, they purified themselves, as the custom was, and kept the sabbath in the same place.

39 And upon the day following, as the use had been, Y'hudah and his company came to take up the bodies of them that were slain, and to bury them with their kinsmen in their fathers' graves.

40 Now under the coats of every one that was slain they found things consecrated to the idols of the Jamnites, which is forbidden the Y'hudim by the Torah. Then every man saw that this was the cause wherefore they were slain.

41 All men therefore praising Elohim[70], the righteous Judge, who had opened the things that were hid,

42 Betook themselves unto prayer, and besought him that the sin committed might wholly be put out of remembrance. Besides, that noble Y'hudah exhorted the people to keep themselves from sin, forsomuch as they saw before their eyes the things that came to pass for the sins of those that were slain.

43 And when he had made a gathering throughout the company to the sum of two thousand drachms of silver, he sent it to Yerushalayim to offer a sin offering, doing therein very well and honestly, in that he was mindful of the resurrection:

44 For if he had not hoped that they that were slain should have risen again, it had been superfluous and vain to pray for the dead.

45 And also in that he perceived that there was great favour laid up for those that died godly, it was an set-apart and good thought.
Whereupon he made a reconciliation for the dead, that they might be delivered from sin.

CHAPTER 13

1 In the hundred forty and ninth year it was told Y'hudah, that Antiochus Eupator was coming with a great power into Y'hudah,

2 And with him Lysias his protector, and ruler of his affairs, having either of them a Greek power of footmen, an hundred and ten thousand, and horsemen five thousand and three hundred, and

---

[70] Aramaic: אלהא "Elohim;Elohim" Greek: Κυριου "Lord"

elephants two and twenty, and three hundred chariots armed with hooks.

3 Menelans also joined himself with them, and with great dissimulation encouraged Antiochus, not for the safeguard of the country, but because he thought to have been made governor.

4 But the King of kings moved Antiochus' mind against this wicked wretch, and Lysias informed the king that this man was the cause of all mischief, so that the king commanded to bring him unto Berea, and to put him to death, as the manner is in that place.

5 Now there was in that place a tower of fifty cubits high, full of ashes, and it had a round instrument which on every side hanged down into the ashes.

6 And whosoever was condemned of sacrilege, or had committed any other grievous crime, there did all men thrust him unto death.

7 Such a death it happened that wicked man to die, not having so much as burial in the earth; and that most justly:

8 For inasmuch as he had committed many sins about the altar, whose fire and ashes were set-apart, he received his death in ashes.

9 Now the king came with a barbarous and haughty mind to do far worse to the Y'hudim, than had been done in his father's time.

10 Which things when Y'hudah perceived, he commanded the multitude to call upon YHWH night and day, that if ever at any other time, he would now also help them, being at the point to be put from their Torah, from their country, and from the set-apart Temple:

11 And that he would not suffer the people, that had even now been but a little refreshed, to be in subjection to the blasphemous nations.

12 So when they had all done this together, and besought the merciful Elohim[71] with weeping and fasting, and lying flat upon the ground three days long, Y'hudah, having exhorted them, commanded they should be in a readiness.

13 And Y'hudah, being apart with the elders, determined, before the king's host should enter into Y'hudah, and get the city, to go forth and try the matter in fight by the help of Elohim[72].

14 So when he had committed all to the Creator of the world, and exhorted his soldiers to fight manfully, even unto death, for the laws, the Temple, the city, the country, and the commonwealth, he camped by Modin:

15 And having given the watchword to them that were about him, Victory is of Elohim; with the most valiant and choice young men he

---

[71] Aramaic: אלהא "Elohim;Elohim" Greek: Κυριου "Lord"

[72] Aramaic: אלהא "Elohim;Elohim" Greek: Κυριου "Lord"

went in into the king's tent by night, and slew in the camp about four thousand men, and the chiefest of the elephants, with all that were upon him.

16 And at last they filled the camp with fear and tumult, and departed with good success.

17 This was done in the break of the day, because the protection of YHWH did help him.

18 Now when the king had taken a taste of the manliness of the Y'hudim, he went about to take the holds by policy,

19 And marched toward Beit-Tzur, which was a strong hold of the Y'hudim: but he was put to flight, failed, and lost of his men:

20 For Y'hudah had conveyed unto them that were in it such things as were necessary.

21 But Rhodocus, who was in the Y'hudim' host, disclosed the secrets to the enemies; therefore he was sought out, and when they had gotten him, they put him in prison.

22 The king treated with them in Bethsum the second time, gave his hand, took their's, departed, fought with Y'hudah, was overcome;

23 Heard that Philip, who was left over the affairs in Antioch, was desperately bent, confounded, intreated the Y'hudim, submitted himself, and sware to all equal conditions, agreed with them, and offered sacrifice, honoured the Temple, and dealt kindly with the place,

24 And accepted well of Maccabee, made him principal governor from Ptolemais unto the Gerrhenians;

25 Came to Ptolemais: the people there were grieved for the covenants; for they stormed, because they would make their covenants void:

26 Lysias went up to the judgment seat, said as much as could be in defence of the cause, persuaded, pacified, made them well affected, returned to Antioch. Thus it went touching the king's coming and departing.

CHAPTER 14

1 After three years was Y'hudah informed, that Demetrius the son of Seleucus, having entered by the haven of Tripolis with a great power and navy,

2 Had taken the country, and killed Antiochus, and Lysias his protector.

3 Now one Alcimus, who had been Cohen Ha-Gadol, and had defiled himself wilfully in the times of their mingling with the Goyim, seeing that by no means he could save himself, nor have any more access to the set-apart altar,

4 Came to king Demetrius in the hundred and one and fiftieth year, presenting unto him a crown of gold, and a palm, and also of the boughs which were used solemnly in the Temple: and so that day he held his peace.

5 Howbeit having gotten opportunity to further his foolish enterprize, and being called into counsel by Demetrius, and asked how the Y'hudim stood affected, and what they intended, he answered thereunto:

6 Those of the Y'hudim that he called Chasidim, whose captain is Y'hudah Maccabee, nourish war and are seditious, and will not let the rest be in peace.

7 Therefore I, being deprived of mine ancestors' honour, I mean the Cohen HaGadolhood, am now come hither:

8 First, verily for the unfeigned care I have of things pertaining to the king; and secondly, even for that I intend the good of mine own countrymen: for all our nation is in no small misery through the unadvised dealing of them aforersaid.

9 Wherefore, O king, seeing know all these things, be careful for the country, and our nation, which is pressed on every side, according to the clemency that you readily show unto all.

10 For as long as Y'hudah lives, it is not possible that the state should be quiet.

11 This was no sooner spoken of him, but others of the king's friends, being maliciously set against Y'hudah, did more incense Demetrius.

12 And forthwith calling Nicanor, who had been master of the elephants, and making him governor over Y'hudah, he sent him forth,

13 Commanding him to slay Y'hudah, and to scatter them that were with him, and to make Alcimus Cohen Ha-Gadol of the great Temple.

14 Then the heathen, that had fled out of Y'hudah from Y'hudah, came to Nicanor by flocks, thinking the harm and calamities of the Y'hudim to be their welfare.

15 Now when the Y'hudim heard of Nicanor's coming, and that the heathen were up against them, they cast earth upon their heads, and made supplication to him that had established his people for ever, and who always helps his portion with manifestation of his presence.

16 So at the commandment of the captain they removed straightways from thence, and came near unto them at the town of Dessau.

17 Now Shim'on, Y'hudah' brother, had joined battle with Nicanor, but was somewhat discomfited through the sudden silence of his enemies.

18 Nevertheless Nicanor, hearing of the manliness of them that were with Y'hudah, and the courageousness that they had to fight for their country, durst not try the matter by the sword.

19 Wherefore he sent Posidonius, and Theodotus, and Mattityahu, to make peace.

20 So when they had taken long advisement thereupon, and the captain had made the multitude acquainted therewith, and it appeared that they were all of one mind, they consented to the covenants,

21 And appointed a day to meet in together by themselves: and when the day came, and stools were set for either of them,

22 Ludas placed armed men ready in convenient places, lest some treachery should be suddenly practised by the enemies: so they made a peaceable conference.

23 Now Nicanor abode in Yerushalayim, and did no hurt, but sent away the people that came flocking unto him.

24 And he would not willingly have Y'hudah out of his sight: for he love the man from his heart

25 He prayed him also to take a wife, and to beget children: so he married, was quiet, and took part of this life.

26 But Alcimus, perceiving the love that was betwixt them, and considering the covenants that were made, came to Demetrius, and told him that Nicanor was not well affected toward the state; for that he had ordained Y'hudah, a traitor to his realm, to be the king's successor.

27 Then the king being in a rage, and provoked with the accusations of the most wicked man, wrote to Nicanor, signifying that he was much displeased with the covenants, and commanding him that he should send Maccabee prisoner in all haste unto Antioch.

28 When this came to Nicanor's hearing, he was much confounded in himself, and took it grievously that he should make void the articles which were agreed upon, the man being in no fault.

29 But because there was no dealing against the king, he watched his time to accomplish this thing by policy.

30 Notwithstanding, when Maccabee saw that Nicanor began to be churlish unto him, and that he entreated him more roughly than he was wont, perceiving that such sour behaviour came not of good, he gathered together not a few of his men, and withdrew himself from Nicanor.

31 But the other, knowing that he was notably prevented by Y'hudah' policy, came into the great and set-apart temple, and commanded the cohenim, that were offering their usual sacrifices, to deliver him the man.

32 And when they sware that they could not tell where the man was whom he sought,

33 He stretched out his right hand toward the Temple, and made an oath in this manner: If you will not deliver me Y'hudah as a prisoner, I will lay this Temple of Elohim even with the ground, and I will break down the altar, and erect a notable temple unto Bacchus.

34 After these words he departed. Then the cohenim lifted up their hands toward heaven, and besought him that was ever a defender of their nation, saying in this manner;

35 You, O YHWH of all things, who have need of nothing, wast pleased that the Temple of Your habitation should be among us:

36 Therefore now, O Set-apart YHWH of all holiness, keep this house ever undefiled, which lately was cleansed, and stop every unrighteous mouth.

37 Now was there accused unto Nicanor one Razis, one of the elders of Yerushalayim, a lover of his countrymen, and a man of very good report, who for his kindness was called a father of the Y'hudim.

38 For in the former times, when they mingled not themselves with the Goyim, he had been accused of Judaism, and did boldly jeopard his body and life with all vehemency for the religion of the Y'hudim.

39 So Nicanor, willing to declare the hate that he bare unto the Y'hudim, sent above five hundred men of war to take him:

40 For he thought by taking him to do the Y'hudim much hurt.

41 Now when the multitude would have taken the tower, and violently broken into the outer door, and bade that fire should be brought to burn it, he being ready to be taken on every side fell upon his sword;

42 Choosing rather to die manfully, than to come into the hands of the wicked, to be abused otherwise than beseemed his noble birth:

43 But missing his stroke through haste, the multitude also rushing within the doors, he ran boldly up to the wall, and cast himself down manfully among the thickest of them.

44 But they quickly giving back, and a space being made, he fell down into the midst of the void place.

45 Nevertheless, while there was yet breath within him, being inflamed with anger, he rose up; and though his blood gushed out like spouts of water, and his wounds were grievous, yet he ran through the midst of the throng; and standing upon a steep rock,

46 When as his blood was now quite gone, he plucked out his bowels, and taking them in both his hands, he cast them upon the throng, and calling upon YHWH of life and spirit to restore him those again, he thus died.

CHAPTER 15

1 But Nicanor, hearing that Y'hudah and his company were in the strong places about Samaria, resolved without any danger to set upon them on the sabbath day.

2 Nevertheless the Y'hudim that were compelled to go with him said, O destroy not so cruelly and barbarously, but give honour to that day, which he, that sees all things, has honoured with holiness above all other days.

3 Then the most ungracious wretch demanded, if there were a Mighty one in heaven, that had commanded the sabbath day to be kept.

4 And when they said, There is in heaven a living YHWH, and mighty, who commanded the seventh day to be kept:

5 Then said the other, And I also am mighty upon earth, and I command to take arms, and to do the king's business. Yet he obtained not to have his wicked will done.

6 So Nicanor in exceeding pride and haughtiness determined to set up a public monument of his victory over Y'hudah and them that were with him.

7 But Maccabee had ever sure confidence that Elohim[73] would help him:

8 Wherefore he exhorted his people not to fear the coming of the heathen against them, but to remember the help which in former times they had received from heaven, and now to expect the victory and aid, which should come unto them from the only Elohim.

9 And so comforting them out of the Torah and the Prophets, and withal putting them in mind of the battles that they won afore, he made them more cheerful.

10 And when he had stirred up their minds, he gave them their charge, shewing them therewithall the falsehood of the heathen, and the breach of oaths.

11 Thus he armed every one of them, not so much with defence of shields and spears, as with comfortable and good words: and beside

---

[73] Aramaic: אלהא "Elohim;Elohim" Greek: Κυριου "Lord"

that, he told them a dream worthy to be believed, as if it had been so indeed, which did not a little rejoice them.

12 And this was his vision: That Onias, who had been Cohen Ha-Gadol, a virtuous and a good man, reverend in conversation, gentle in condition, well spoken also, and exercised from a child in all points of virtue, holding up his hands prayed for the whole body of the Y'hudim.

13 This done, in like manner there appeared a man with gray hairs, and exceeding glorious, who was of a wonderful and excellent majesty.

14 Then Onias answered, saying, This is a lover of the brothers, who prays much for the people, and for the set-apart city, to wit, Yirmeyahu the prophet of Elohim.

15 Whereupon Yirmeyahu holding forth his right hand gave to Y'hudah a sword of gold, and in giving it spake thus,

16 Take this set-apart sword, a gift from Elohim, with the which you shall wound the adversaries.

17 Thus being well comforted by the words of Y'hudah, which were very good, and able to stir them up to valour, and to encourage the hearts of the young men, they determined not to pitch camp, but courageously to set upon them, and manfully to try the matter by conflict, because the city and the sanctuary and the Temple were in danger.

18 For the care that they took for their wives, and their children, their brothers, and folks, was in least account with them: but the greatest and principal fear was for the set-apart Temple.

19 Also they that were in the city took not the least care, being troubled for the conflict abroad.

20 And now, when as all looked what should be the trial, and the enemies were already come near, and the army was set in array, and the beasts conveniently placed, and the horsemen set in wings,

21 Maccabee seeing the coming of the multitude, and the divers preparations of armour, and the fierceness of the beasts, stretched out his hands toward heaven, and called upon Elohim[74] that works wonders, knowing that victory comes not by arms, but even as it seems good to him, he gives it to such as are worthy:

22 Therefore in his prayer he said after this manner; O YHWH, you did send your angel in the time of Yechezk'el king of Y'hudah, and did slay in the host of Sennacherib an hundred fourscore and five thousand[75]:

---

[74] Aramaic: אלהא "Elohim;Elohim" Greek: Κυριου "Lord"
[75] 2Kn. 19:35

23 Wherefore now also, O YHWH of heaven, send a good angel before us for a fear and dread unto them;

24 And through the might of your arm let those be stricken with terror, that come against your set-apart people to blaspheme. And he ended thus.

25 Then Nicanor and they that were with him came forward with trumpets and songs.

26 But Y'hudah and his company encountered the enemies with invocation and prayer.

27 So that fighting with their hands, and praying unto Elohim with their hearts, they slew no less than thirty and five thousand men: for through the appearance of Elohim they were greatly cheered.

28 Now when the battle was done, returning again with joy, they knew that Nicanor lay dead in his harness.

29 Then they made a great shout and a noise, praising YHWH[76] in their own language.

30 And Y'hudah, who was ever the chief defender of the citizens both in body and mind, and who continued his love toward his countrymen all his life, commanded to strike off Nicanor's head, and his hand with his shoulder, and bring them to Yerushalayim.

31 So when he was there, and called them of his nation together, and set the cohenim before the altar, he sent for them that were of the tower,

32 And showed them vile Nicanor's head, and the hand of that blasphemer, which with proud brags he had stretched out against the Set-apart Temple of the only Elohim.

33 And when he had cut out the tongue of that ungodly Nicanor, he commanded that they should give it by pieces unto the fowls, and hang up the reward of his madness before the Temple.

34 So every man praised toward the heaven the glorious YHWH, saying, Blessed be he that has kept his own place undefiled.

35 He hanged also Nicanor's head upon the tower, an evident and manifest sign unto all of the help of our Elohim[77].

36 And they ordained all with a common decree in no case to let that day pass without solemnity, but to celebrate the thirtieth day of the twelfth month, which in the Syrian tongue is called Adar, the day before Mordekhai's day[78].

---

[76] Following the Aramaic, the Greek has "the Almighty"

[77] "our Elohim" following the Aramaic. The Greek has "the Lord".

[78] Ester 920-32

37 Thus went it with Nicanor: and from that time forth the Hebrews had the city in their power. And here will I make an end.

38 And if I have done well, and as is fitting the story, it is that which I desired: but if slenderly and meanly, it is that which I could attain unto.

39 For as it is hurtful to drink wine or water alone; and as wine mingled with water is pleasant, and delights the taste: even so speech finely framed delights the ears of them that read the story. And here shall be an end.

ספר מקבים ג
3Maccabim

CHAPTER 1

1 Now Philopater, on learning from those who came back that
Antiochus had made himself master of the places which belonged to
himself, sent orders to all his footmen and horsemen, took with him his
sister Arsinoe, and marched out as far as the parts of Raphia, where
Antiochus and his forces encamped.

2 And one Theodotus, intending to carry out his design, took with him
the bravest of the armed men who had been before committed to his
trust by Ptolemy, and got through at night to the tent of Ptolemy, to kill
him on his own responsibility, and so to end the war.

3 But Dositheus, called the son of Drimulus, by birth a Jew, afterward
a renegade from the laws and observances of his country, conveyed
Ptolemy away, and made an obscure person lie down in his stead in the
tent. It befell this man to receive the fate which was meant for the
other.

4 A fierce battle then took place; and the men of Antiochus prevailing,
Arsinoe continually went up and down the ranks, and with dishevelled
hair, with tears and entreaties, begged the soldiers to fight manfully for
themselves, their children, and wives; and promised that if they proved
conquerors, she would give them two minae of gold apiece.

5 It thus fell out that their enemies were defeated in hand-to-hand
encounter, and that many of them were taken prisoners.

6 Having vanquished this attempt, the king then decided to proceed to
the neighbouring cities, and encourage them.

7 By doing this, and by making donations to their temples, he inspired
his subjects with confidence.

8 The Jews sent some of their council and of their elders to him. The
greetings, guest-gifts, and congratulations of the past, bestowed by
them, filled him with the greater eagerness to visit their city.

9 Having arrived at Yerushalayim, sacrificed, and offered thank-
offerings to the Greatest Elohim, and done whatever else was suitable
to the sanctity of the place, and entered the inner court,

10 he was so struck with the magnificence of the place, and so
wondered at the orderly arrangements of the temple, that he considered
entering the sanctuary itself.

11 And when they told him that this was not permissible, none of the nation, no, nor even the priests in general, but only the supreme Cohen HaGadol of all, and he only once in a year, being allowed to go in[79], he would by no means give way.

12 Then they read the Torah to him; but he persisted in obtruding himself, exclaiming, that he ought to be allowed: and saying Be it that they were deprived of this honour, I ought not to be.

13 And he put the question, Why, when he entered all the temples, none of the priests who were present forbad him?

14 He was thoroughly answered by some one, That he did wrong to boast of this.

15 Well; since I have done this, said he, be the cause what it may, shall I not enter with or without your consent?

16 And when the priests fell down in their sacred vestments imploring the Greatest Elohim to come and help in time of need, and to avert the violence of the fierce aggressor, and when they filled the temple with lamentations and tears,

17 then those who had been left behind in the city were scared, and rushed forth, uncertain of the event.

18 Virgins, who had been shut up within their chambers, came out with their mothers, scattering dust and ashes on their heads, and filling the streets with outcries.

19 Women, but recently separated off, left their bridal chambers, left the reserve that befitted them, and ran about the city in a disorderly manner.

20 New-born babes were deserted by the mothers or nurses who waited upon them; some here, some there, in houses, or in fields; these now, with an ardour which could not be checked, swarmed into the Most High Temple.

21 Various were the prayers offered up by those who assembled in this place, on account of the unholy attempt of the king.

22 Along with these there were some of the citizens who took courage, and would not submit to his obstinacy, and his intention of carrying out his purpose.

23 Calling out to arms, and to die bravely in defence of the Torah of their fathers, they created a great uproar in the place, and were with difficulty brought back by the aged and the elders to the station of prayer which they had occupied before.

24 During this time the multitude kept on praying.

---

[79] Ex. 30:10; Lev. 16:2, 11-12, 15, 34; Heb. 9:7

25 The elders who surrounded the king strove in many ways to divert his haughty mind from the design which he had formed.

26 He, in his hardened mood, insensible to all persuasion, was going onwards with the view of carrying out this design.

27 Yet even his own officers, when they saw this, joined the Jews in an appeal to Him who has all power, to aid in the present crisis, and not wink at such overweening lawlessness[80].

28 Such was the frequency and the vehemence of the cry of the assembled crowd, that an indescribable noise ensued.

29 Not the men only, but the very walls and floor seemed to sound forth; all things preferring dissolution rather than to see the place defiled.

CHAPTER 2

1 Now was it that the Cohen HaGadol Shim'om bowed his knees over against the Set-apart Place, and spread out his hands in reverent form, and uttered the following supplication:

2 O YHWH, YHWH, King of the heavens, and Ruler of the whole creation, Set-apart among the set-apart, sole Governor, Almighty, give ear to us who are oppressed by a wicked and profane one, who exults in his confidence and strength.

3 It is you, the Creator of all, the Master of the universe, who are a righteous Governor, and judge all who act with pride and insolence.

4 It was you who did destroy the former workers of unrighteousness, among whom were the giants, who trusted in their strength and hardihood, by covering them with a measureless flood[81].

5 It was you who did make the Sodomites, those workers of exceeding iniquity, men notorious for their vices, an example to after generations, when you did cover them with fire and brimstone.[82]

6 You did make known your power when you caused the bold Pharaoh, the enslaver of your people, to pass through the ordeal of many and diverse inflictions.[83]

7 And you rolled the depths of the sea over him, when he made pursuit with chariots, and with a multitude of followers, and gave a safe

---

[80] Greek: ανομον from the Greek prefix α- "without" and νομον
[81] Gen. 6:4-7; 7; 1En. 7:2; 15:8
[82] Gen. 19:24
[83] Ex. 5-12

passage to those who put their trust in you, the Master of the whole creation[84].

8 These saw and felt the works of your hands, and praised you the Almighty.

9 You, O King, when you created the illimitable and measureless earth, did choose out this city: you did make this place sacred to your name, albeit you need nothing: you did glorify it with your illustrious presence, after constructing it to the glory of your great and honourable name.

10 And you did promise, out of love to the people of Yisrael, that should we fall away from you, and become afflicted, and then come to this house and pray, you would hear our prayer[85].

11 Verily you are faithful and true.

12 And when you did often aid our fathers when hard pressed, and in low estate, and deliveredst them out of great dangers,

13 see now, set-apart King, how through our many and great sins we are borne down, and made subject to our enemies, and are become weak and powerless.

14 We being in this low condition, this bold and profane man seeks to dishonour this your set-apart place, consecrated out of the earth to the name of your Majesty.

15 Your dwelling place, the heaven of heavens, is indeed unapproachable to men.

16 But since it seemed good to you to exhibit your glory among your people Yisrael, you did sanctify this place[86].

17 Punish us not by means of the uncleanness of their men, nor chastise us by means of their profanity; lest the opposers of Torah[87] should boast in their rage, and exult in exuberant pride of speech, and say,

18 We have trampled upon the set-apart house, as idolatrous houses are trampled upon.

19 Blot out our iniquities, and do away with our errors, and show forth your compassion in this hour.

20 Let your mercies quickly go before us. Grant us shalom, that the cast down and broken hearted may praise you with their mouth.

---

[84] Ex. 14:21-31

[85] 1Kn. 8:33-53

[86] 1Kn. 8:27-29

[87] Greek: παρανομοι "opposers of Torah" from the Greek prefix παρα "to oppose" and the Greek word νομος "Torah".

21 At that time Elohim, who sees all things, who is beyond all Set-apart among the set-apart, heard that prayer, so suitable; and scourged the man greatly uplifted with scorn and insolence.

22 Shaking him to and fro as a reed is shaken with the wind, he cast him upon the pavement, powerless, with limbs paralyzed; by a righteous judgment deprived of the faculty of speech.

23 His friends and bodyguards, beholding the swift recompense which had suddenly overtaken him, struck with exceeding terror, and fearing that he would die, speedily removed him.

24 When in course of time he had come to himself, this severe check caused no repentance within him, but he departed with bitter threatenings.

25 He proceeded to Egypt, grew worse in wickedness through his before mentioned companions in wine, who were lost to all goodness;

26 and not satisfied with countless acts of impiety, his audacity so increased that he raised evil reports there, and many of his friends, watching his purpose attentively, joined in furthering his will.

27 His purpose was to indict a public stigma upon our race; wherefore he erected a pillar at the towerporch, and caused the following inscription to be engraved upon it:

28 That entrance to their own temple was to be refused to all those who would not sacrifice; that all the Jews were to be registered among the common people; that those who resisted were to be forcibly seized and put to death;

29 that those who were thus registered, were to be marked on their persons by the ivyleaf symbol of Dionysus, and to be set apart with these limited rights.

30 To do away with the appearance of hating them all, he had it written underneath, that if any of them should elect to enter the community of those initiated in the rites, these should have equal rights with the Alexandrians.

31 Some of those who were over the city, therefore, abhorring any approach to the city of piety, unhesitatingly gave in to the king, and expected to derive some great honour from a future connection with him.

32 A nobler spirit, however, prompted the majority to cling to their religious observances, and by paying money that they might live unmolested, these sought to escape the registration:

33 cheerfully looking forward to future aid, they abhorred their own apostates, considering them to be national foes, and debarring them from the common usages of social intercourse.

CHAPTER 3

1 On discovering this, so incensed was the wicked king, that he no longer confined his rage to the Jews in Alexandria. Laying his hand more heavily upon those who lived in the country, he gave orders that they should be quickly collected into one place, and most cruelly deprived of their lives.

2 While this was going on, an invidious rumour was uttered abroad by men who had banded together to injure the Jewish race. The purport of their charge was, that the Jews kept them away from the ordinances of the Torah.

3 Now, while the Jews always maintained a feeling of un-swerving loyalty towards the kings,

4 yet, as they worshipped Elohim, and observed his Torah, they made certain distinctions, and avoided certain things. Hence some persons held them in odium;

5 although, as they adorned their conversation with works of righteousness, they had established themselves in the good opinion of the world.

6 What all the rest of mankind said, was, however, made of no account by the foreigners;

7 who said much of the exclusiveness of the Jews with regard to their worship and meats; they alleged that they were men unsociable, hostile to the king's interests, refusing to associate with him or his troops. By this way of speaking, they brought much odium upon them.

8 Nor was this unexpected uproar and sudden conflux of people unobserved by the Greeks who lived in the city, concerning men who had never harmed them: yet to aid them was not in their power, since all was oppression around; but they encouraged them in their troubles, and expected a favourable turn of affairs:

9 He who knows all things, will not, [said they,] disregard so great a people.

10 Some of the neighbors, friends, and fellow dealers of the Jews, even called them secretly to an interview, pledged them their assistance, and promised to do their very utmost for them.

11 Now the king, elated with his prosperous fortune, and not regarding the superior power of Elohim, but thinking to persevere in his present purpose, wrote the following letter to the prejudice of the Jews.

12 King Ptolemy Philopater, to the commanders and soldiers in Egypt, and in all places, health and happiness!

13 I am right well; and so, too, are my affairs.

14 Since our Asiatic campaign, the particulars of which you know, and which by the aid of the gods, not lightly given, and by our own vigour, has been brought to a successful issue according to our expectation,

15 we resolved, not with strength of spear, but with gentleness and much humanity, as it were to nurse the inhabitants of Coele-Syria and Phoenicia, and to be their willing benefactors.

16 So, having bestowed considerable sums of money upon the temples of the several cities, we proceeded even as far as Yerushalayim; and went up to honour the temple of these wretched beings who never cease from their folly.

17 To outward appearance they received us willingly; but belied that appearance by their deeds. When we were eager to enter their temple, and to honour it with the most beautiful and exquisite gifts,

18 they were so carried away by their old arrogance, as to forbid us the entrance; while we, out of our forbearance toward all men, refrained from exercising our power upon them.

19 And thus, exhibiting their enmity against us, they alone among the nations lift up their heads against kings and benefactors, as men unwilling to submit to any thing reasonable.

20 We then, having endeavoured to make allowance for the madness of these persons, and on our victorious return treating all people in Egypt courteously, acted in a manner which was befitting.

21 Accordingly, bearing no ill-will against their kinsmen [at Yerushalayim,] but rather remembering our connection with them, and the numerous matters with sincere heart from a remote period entrusted to them, we wished to venture a total alteration of their state, by bestowing upon them the rights of citizens of Alexandria, and to admit them to the everlasting rites of our solemnities.

22 All this, however, they have taken in a very different spirit. With their innate malignity, they have spurned the fair offer; and constantly inclining to evil,

23 have rejected the inestimable rights. Not only so, but by using speech, and by refraining from speech, they abhor the few among them who are heartily disposed towards us; ever deeming that their ignoble course of procedure will force us to do away with our reform.

24 Having then, received certain proofs that these [Jews] bear us every sort of ill-will, we must look forward to the possibility of some sudden tumult among ourselves, when these impious men may turn traitors and barbarous enemies.

25 As soon, therefore, as the contents of this letter become known to you, in that same hour we order those [Jews] who dwell among you, with wives and children, to be sent to us, vilified and abused, in chains

of iron, to undergo a death, cruel and ignominious, suitable to men disaffected.

26 For by the punishment of them in one body we perceive that we have found the only means of establishing our affairs for the future on a firm and satisfactory basis.

27 Whosoever shall shield a Jew, whether it be old man, child, or suckling, shall with his whole house be tortured to death.

28 Whoever shall inform against the [Jews,] besides receiving the property of the person charged, shall be presented with two thousand drachmae from the royal treasury, shall be made free, and shall be crowned.

29 Whatever place shall shelter a Jew, shall, when he is hunted forth, be put under the ban of fire, and be for ever rendered useless to every living being for all time to come.

30 Such was the purport of the king's letter.

CHAPTER 4

1 Wherever this decree was received, the people kept up a revelry of joy and shouting; as if their long-pent-up, hardened hatred, were now to shew itself openly.

2 The Jews suffered great throes of sorrow, and wept much; while their hearts, all things around being lamentable, were set on fire as they bewailed the sudden destruction which was decreed against them.

3 What home, or city, or place at all inhabited, or what streets were there, which their condition did not fill with wailing and lamentation?

4 They were sent out unanimously by the generals in the several cities, with such stern and pitiless feeling, that the exceptional nature of the infliction moved even some of their enemies. These, influenced by sentiments of common humanity, and reflecting upon
the uncertain issue of life, shed tears at this their miserable expulsion.

5 A multitude of aged hoary-haired old men, were driven along with halting bending feet, urged onward by the impulse of a violent, shameless force to quick speed.

6 Girls who had entered the bridal chamber quite lately, to enjoy the partnership of marriage, exchanged pleasure for misery; and with dust scattered upon their myrrh-anointed heads, were hurried along unveiled; and, in the midst of outlandish insults, set up with one accord a lamentable cry in lieu of the marriage hymn.

7 Bound, and exposed to public gaze, they were hurried violently on board ship.

8 The husbands of these, in the prime of their youthful vigour, instead of crowns wore halters round their necks; instead of feasting and youthful jollity, spent the rest of their nuptial days in wailings, and saw only the grave at hand.

9 They were dragged along by unyielding chains, like wild beasts: of these, some had their necks thrust into the benches of the rowers; while the feet of others were enclosed in hard fetters.

10 The planks of the deck above them barred out the light, and shut out the day on every side, so that they might be treated like traitors during the whole voyage.

11 They were conveyed accordingly in this vessel, and at the end of it arrived at Schedia. The king had ordered them to be cast into the vast hippodrome, which was built in front of the city. This place was well adapted by its situation to expose them to the gaze of all comers into the city, and of those who went from the city into the country. Thus they could

hold no communication with his forces; nay, were deemed unworthy of any civilized accommodation.

12 When this was done, the king, hearing that their brothers in the city often went out and lamented the melancholy distress of these victims,

13 was full of rage, and commanded that they should be carefully subjected to the same (and not one whit milder) treatment.

14 The whole nation was now to be registered. Every individual was to be specified by name; not for that hard servitude of labour which we have a little before mentioned, but that he might expose them to the before-mentioned tortures; and finally, in the short space of a day, might extirpate them by his cruelties.

15 The registering of these men was carried on cruelly, zealously, assiduously, from the rising of the sun to its going down, and was not brought to an end in forty days.

16 The king was filled with great and constant joy, and celebrated banquets before the temple idols. His erring heart, far from the truth, and his profane mouth, gave glory to idols, deaf and incapable of speaking or aiding, and uttered unworthy speech against the Greatest Elohim.

17 At the end of the above-mentioned interval of time, the registrars brought word to the king that the multitude of the Jews was too great for registration,

18 inasmuch as there were many still left in the land, of whom some were in inhabited houses, and others were scattered about in various places; so that all the commanders in Egypt were insufficient for the work.

19 The king threatened them, and charged them with taking bribes, in order to contrive the escape of the Jews: but was clearly convinced of the truth of what had been said.

20 They said, and proved, that paper and pens had failed them for the carrying out of their purpose.

21 Now this was an active interference of the unconquerable Providence which assisted the Jews from heaven.

CHAPTER 5

1 Then he called Hermon, who had charge of the elephants. Full of rage, altogether fixed in his furious design,

2 he commanded him, with a quantity of unmixed wine and handfuls of incense [infused] to drug the elephants early on the following day. These five hundred elephants were, when infuriated by the copious draughts of frankincense, to be led up to the execution of death upon the Jews.

3 The king, after issuing these orders, went to his feasting, and gathered together all those of his friends and of the army who hated the Jews the most.

4 The master of the elephants, Hermon, fulfilled his commission punctually.

5 The underlings appointed for the purpose went out about eventide and bound the hands of the miserable victims, and took other precautions for their security at night, thinking that the whole race would perish together.

6 The heathen believed the Jews to be destitute of all protection; for chains fettered them about.

7 they invoked the Almighty YHWH, and ceaselessly besought with tears their merciful Elohim and Father, Ruler of all, Master of every power,

8 to overthrow the evil purpose which was gone out against them, and to deliver them by extraordinary manifestation from that death which was in store for them.

9 their litany so earnest went up to heaven.

10 Then Hermon, who had filled his merciless elephants with copious draughts of mingled wine and frankincense, came early to the palace to certify the kind thereof.

11 He, however, who has sent his good creature sleep from all time by night or by day thus gratifying whom he wills, diffused a portion thereof now upon the king.

12 By this sweet and profound influence of YHWH he was held fast, and thus his unjust purpose was quite frustrated, and his unflinching resolve greatly falsified.

13 But the Jews, having escaped the hour which had been fixed, praised their set-apart Elohim, and again prayed him who is easily reconciled to display the power of his powerful hand to the overweening Goyim.

14 The middle of the tenth hour had well nigh arrived, when the master-bidder, seeing the guests who were bidden collected, came and shook the king.

15 He gained his attention with difficulty, and hinting that the mealtime was getting past, talked the matter over with him.

16 The kind listened to this, and then turning aside to his potations, commanded the guests to sit down before him.

17 This done, he asked them to enjoy themselves, and to indulge in mirth at this somewhat late hour of the banquet.

18 Conversation grew on, and the king sent for Hermon, and enquired of him, with fierce denunciations, why the Jews had been allowed to outlive that day.

19 Hermon explained that he had done his bidding over night; and in this he was confirmed by his friends.

20 The king, then, with a barbarity exceeding that of Phalaris, said, That they might thank his sleep of that day. Lose no time, and get ready the elephants against tomorrow, as you did before, for the destruction of these accursed Jews.

21 When the king said this, the company present were glad, and approved; and then each man went to his own home.

22 Nor did they employ the night in sleep, so much as in contriving cruel mockeries for those deemed miserable.

23 The morning cock had just crowed, and Hermon, having harnessed the brutes, was stimulating them in the great colonnade.

24 The city crowds were collected together to see the hideous spectacle, and waited impatiently for the dawn.

25 The Jews, breathless with momentary suspense, stretched forth their hands, and prayed the Greatest Elohim, in mournful strains, again to help them speedily.

26 The sun's rays were not yet shed abroad, and the king was waiting for his friends, when Hermon came to him, calling him out, and saying, That his desires could now be realized.

27 The king, receiving him, was astonished at his unwonted exit; and, overwhelmed with a spirit of oblivion about everything, enquired the object of this earnest preparation.

28 But this was the working of that Almighty Elohim who had made him forget all his purpose.

29 Hermon, and all his friends, pointed out the preparation of the animals. They are ready, O king, according to your own strict injunction.

30 The king was filled with fierce anger at these words; for, by the Providence of Elohim regarding these things, his mind had become entirely confused. He looked hard
at Hermon, and threatened him as follows:

31 Your parents, or your children, were they here, to these wild beasts a large repast they should have furnished; not these innocent Jews, who me and my forefathers loyally have served.

32 Had it not been for familiar friendship, and the claims of your office, your life should have gone for theirs.

33 Hermon, being threatened in this unexpected and alarming manner, was troubled in visage, and depressed in countenance.

34 The friends, too, stole out one by one, and dismissed the assembled multitudes to their respective occupations.

35 The Jews, having heard of these events, praised the glorious Elohim and King of kings, because they had obtained this help, too, from him.

36 Now the king arranged another banquet after the same manner, and proclaimed an invitation to mirth.

37 And he summoned Hermon to his presence, and said, with threats, How often, O wretch, must I repeat my orders to you about these same persons?

38 Once more, arm the elephants against the morrow for the extermination of the Jews.

39 His kinsmen, who were reclining with him, wondered at his instability, and thus expressed themselves:

40 O king, how long dost you make trial of us, as of men bereft of reason? This is the third time that you have ordered their destruction. When the thing is to be done, you change your mind, and recall your instructions.

41 For this cause the feeling of expectation causes tumult in the city: it swarms with factions; and is continually on the point of being plundered.

42 The king, just like another Phalaris, a prey to thoughtlessness, made no account of the changes which his own mind had undergone, issuing in the deliverance of the Jews. He swore a fruitless oath, and determined forthwith to send them to hades, crushed by the knees and feet of the elephants.

43 He would also invade Judea, and level its towns with fire and the sword; and destroy that temple which the heathen might not enter, and prevent sacrifices ever after being offered up there.

44 Joyfully his friends broke up, together with his kinsmen; and, trusting in his determination, arranged their forces in guard at the most convenient places of the city.

45 And the master of the elephants urged the beasts into an almost maniacal state, drenched them with incense and wine, and decked them with frightful instruments.

46 About early morning, when the city was now filled with an immense number of people at the hippodrome, he entered the palace, and called the king to the business in hand.

47 The king's heart teemed with impious rage; and he rushed forth with the mass, along with the elephants. With feelings unsoftened, and eyes pitiless, he longed to gaze at the hard and wretched doom of the abovementioned [Jews].

48 But the [Jews,] when the elephants went out at the gate, followed by the armed force; and when they saw the dust raised by the throng, and heard the loud cries of the crowd,

49 thought that they had come to the last moment of their lives, to the end of what they had tremblingly expected. They gave way, therefore, to lamentations and moans: they kissed each other: those nearest of kin to each other hung about one another's necks: fathers about their sons, mother their daughters: other women held their infants to their breasts, which drew what seemed their last milk.

50 Nevertheless, when they reflected upon the succour before granted them from heaven, they prostrated themselves with one accord; removed even the sucking children from the breasts, and

51 sent up an exceeding great cry entreating YHWH of all power to reveal himself, and have mercy upon those who now lay at the gates of hades.

CHAPTER 6

1 And El'azar, an illustrious cohen of the country, who had attained to length of days, and whose life had been adorned with virtue, caused the Elders who were about him to cease to cry out to the set-apart Elohim, and prayed thus:

2 O king, mighty in power, most high, Almighty Elohim, who regulate the whole creation with your tender mercy,

3 look upon the seed of Avraham, upon the children of the sanctified Ya'akov, your sanctified inheritance, O Father, now being wrongfully destroyed as strangers in a strange land.

4 You destroyed Pharaoh, with his hosts of chariots, when that master of this same Egypt was uplifted with Torah-less[88] hardihood and loud-sounding tongue. Shedding the beams of your mercy upon the race of Yisrael, you did overwhelm him with his proud army.[89]

5 When Sennacherim, the grievous king of the Assyrians, glorying in his countless hosts, had subdued the whole land with his spear, and was lifting himself against your set-apart city, with boastings grievous to be endured, you, O YHWH, did demolish him and did shew forth your might to many nations[90].

6 When the three friends in the land of Babylon of their own will exposed their lives to the fire rather than serve vain things, you did send a dewy coolness through the fiery furnace, and bring the fire upon all their adversaries[91].

7 It was you who, when Daniel was hurled, through slander and envy, as a prey to lions down below, did bring him back against unhurt to light[92].

8 When Yonah was pining away in the belly of the sea-bred monster, you did look upon him, O Father, and recover him to the sight of his own[93].

9 And now, you who hate insolence; you who dost abound in mercy; you who are the protector of all things; appear quickly to those of the race of Yisrael, who are insulted by abhorred, Torah-less[94] goyim.

10 If our life has during our exile been stained with iniquity, deliver us from the hand of the enemy, and destroy us, O YHWH, by the death which you prefer.

11 Let not the vain-minded congratulate vain idols at the destruction of your beloved, saying, Neither did their god deliver them.

12 You, who are Allpowerful and Almighty, O Eternal One, behold! have mercy upon us who are being withdrawn from life, like traitors, by the unreasoning insolence of Torah-less[95] men.

---

[88] Greek: ανομω from the Greek prefix α- (without) and the Greek word νομων "Torah"

[89] Ex. 14:28; 15

[90] 2Kn. 18:13; 19:35-37

[91] Dan. 3:22, 27, 50

[92] Dan. 6:24

[93] Jonah 1:17-2:10

[94] Greek: ανομων from the Greek prefix α- (without) and the Greek word νομων "Torah"

13 Let the heathen cower before your invincible might today, O glorious One, who have all power to save the race of Ya'akov.

14 The whole band of infants and their parents with tears beseech you.

15 Let it be shewn to all the nations that you are with us, O YHWH, and have not turned your face away from us; but as you saidst that you wouldst not forget them even in the land of their enemies, so do you fulfil this saying, O YHWH.[96]

16 Now, at the time that El'azar had ended his prayer, the king came along to the hippodrome, with the wild beasts, and with his tumultuous power.

17 When the Jews saw this, they uttered a loud cry to heaven, so that the adjacent valleys resounded, and caused an irrepressible lamentation throughout the army.

18 Then the all-glorious, all-powerful, and true Elohim, displayed his set-apart countenance, and opened the gates of heaven, from which two angels, dreadful of form, came down and were visible to all but the Jews.

19 And they stood opposite, and filled the enemies' host with confusion and cowardice; and bound them with immoveable fetters.

20 And a cold shudder came over the person of the king, and oblivion paralysed the vehemence of his spirit.

21 They turned back the animals upon the armed forces which followed them; and the animals trod them down, and destroyed them.

22 The king's wrath was converted into compassion; and he wept at his own machinations.

23 For when he heard the cry, and saw them all on the verge of destruction, with tears he angrily threatened his friends, saying,

24 Ye have governed badly; and have exceeded tyrants in cruelty; and me your benefactor you have laboured to deprive at once of my dominion and my life, by secretly devising measures injurious to the kingdom.

25 Who has gathered here, unreasonably removing each from his home, those who, in fidelity to us, had held the fortresses of the country?

26 Who has thus consigned to unmerited punishments those who in good will towards us from the beginning have in all things surpassed all nations, and who often have engaged in the most dangerous undertakings?

---

[95] ανομων from the Greek prefix α- (without) and the Greek word νομων "Torah"
[96] Lev. 26:44

27 Loose, loose the unjust bonds; send them to their homes in peace, and deprecate what has been done.

28 Release the sons of the almighty living Elohim of heaven, who from our ancestors' times until now has granted a glorious and uninterrupted prosperity to our affairs.

29 These things he said; and they, released the same moment, having now escaped death, praised Elohim their set-apart Saviour.

30 The king then departed to the city, and called his financier to him, and bade him provide a seven days' quantity of wine and other materials for feasting for the Jews. He decided that they should keep a gladsome festival of deliverance in the very place in which they expected to meet with their destruction.

31 Then they who were before despised and nigh unto hades, yea, rather advanced into it, partook of the cup of salvation, instead of a grievous and lamentable death. Full of exultation, they parted out the place intended for their fall and burial into banqueting booths.

32 Ceasing their miserable strain of woe, they took up the subject of their fatherland, hymning in praise Elohim their wonder-working Saviour. All groans, all wailing, were laid aside: they formed dances in token of serene joy.

33 So, also, the king collected a number of guests for the occasion, and returned unceasing thanks with much magnificence for the unexpected deliverance afforded him.

34 Those who had marked them out as for death and for carrion, and had registered them with joy, howled aloud, and were clothed with shame, and had the fire of their rage ingloriously put out.

35 But the Jews, as we just said, instituted a dance, and then gave themselves up to feasting, glad thanksgivings, and psalms.

36 They made a public ordinance to commemorate these things for generations to come, as long as they should be sojourners. They thus established these days as days of mirth, not for the purpose of drinking or luxury, but because Elohim had saved them.

37 They requested the king to send them back to their homes.

38 They were being enrolled from the twenty-fifth of Pachon to the fourth of Epiphi, a period of forty days: the measures taken for their destruction lasted from the fifth of Epiphi till the seventh, that is, three days.

39 The Ruler over all did during this time manifest forth his mercy gloriously, and did deliver them all together unharmed.

40 They feasted upon the king's provision up to the fourteenth day, and then asked to be sent away.

41 The king commended them, and wrote the subjoined letter, of magnanimous import for them, to the commanders of every city.

CHAPTER 7

1 King Ptolemy Philopator to the commanders throughout Egypt, and to all who are set over affairs, joy and strength.
2 We, too, and our children are well; and Elohim has directed our affairs as we wish.
3 Certain of our friends did of malice vehemently urge us to punish the Jews of our realm in a body, with the infliction of a monstrous punishment.
4 They pretended that our affairs would never be in a good state till this took place. Such, they said, was the hatred borne by the Jews to all other people.
5 They brought them fettered in grievous chains as slaves, nay, as traitors. Without enquiry or examination they endeavoured to annihilate them. They buckled themselves with a savage cruelty, worse than Scythian custom.
6 For this cause we severely threatened them; yet, with the clemency which we are wont to extend to all men, we at length permitted them to live. Finding that the Elohim of heaven cast a shield of protection over the Jews so as to preserve them, and that he fought for them as a father always fights for his sons;
7 and taking into consideration their constancy and fidelity towards us and towards our ancestors, we have, as we ought, acquitted them of every sort of charge.
8 And we have dismissed them to their several homes; bidding all men everywhere to do them no wrong, or unrighteously revile them about the past.
9 For know you, that should we conceive any evil design, or in any way aggrieve them, we shall ever have as our opposite, not man, but the highest Elohim, the ruler of all might. From Him there will be no escape, as the avenger of such deeds. Fare you well.
10 When they had received this letter, they were not forward to depart immediately. They petitioned the king to be allowed to inflict fitting punishment upon those of their race who had willingly transgressed the set-apart Elohim, and the Torah of Elohim.
11 They alleged that men who had for their bellies' sake transgressed the ordinances of Elohim, would never be faithful to the interests of the king.

12 The king admitted the truth of this reasoning, and commended them. Full power was given them, without warrant or special commission, to destroy those who had transgressed the Torah of Elohim boldly in every part of the king's dominions.

13 Their priests, then, as it was meet, saluted him with good wishes, and all the people echoed with the Halleluyah. They then joyfully departed.

14 Then they punished and destroyed with ignominy every polluted Jew that fell in their way;

15 slaying thus, in that day, above three hundred men, and esteeming this destruction of the wicked a season of joy.

16 They themselves having held fast their Elohim unto death, and having enjoyed a full deliverance, departed from the city garlanded with sweet-flowered wreaths of every kind. Uttering exclamations of joy, with songs of praise, and melodious hymns they thanked the Elohim of their fathers, the eternal Saviour of Yisrael.

17 Having arrived at Ptolemais, called from the specialty of that district Rose-bearing, where the fleet, in accordance with the general wish, waited for them seven days,

18 they partook of a banquet of deliverance, for the king generously granted them severally the means of securing a return home.

19 They were accordingly brought back in shalom, while they gave utterance to becoming thanks; and they determined to keep these days during their sojourn as days of joyfulness.

20 These they registered as sacred upon a pillar, when they had dedicated the place of their festivity to be one of prayer. They departed unharmed, free, abundant in joy, preserved by the king's command, by land, by sea, and by river, each to his own home.

21 They had more weight than before among their enemies; and were honoured and feared, and no one in any way robbed them of their goods.

22 Every man received back his own, according to inventory; those who had obtained their goods, giving them up with the greatest terror. For the greatest Elohim wrought with perfectness wonders for their salvation.

23 Blessed be the Redeemer of Yisrael unto everlasting. Amen.

ספר מקבים ד
4Maccabim

CHAPTER 1

1 As I am going to demonstrate a most philosophical proposition, namely, that religious reasoning is absolute master of the passions, I would willingly advise you to give the utmost heed to philosophy.

2 For reason[97] is necessary to every one as a step to knowledge: and more especially does it embrace the praise of prudence, the highest virtue.

3 If, then, reasoning appears to hold the mastery over the passions which stand in the way of temperance, such as gluttony and lust,

4 it surely also and manifestly has the rule over the affections which are contrary to justice, such as malice; and of those which are hindrances to manliness, as wrath, and pain, and fear.

5 How, then, is it, perhaps some may say, that reasoning, if it rule the affections, is not also master of forgetfulness and ignorance? They attempt a ridiculous argument.

6 For reasoning does not rule over its own affections, but over such as are contrary to justice, and manliness and temperance, and prudence; and yet over these, so as to withstand, without destroying them.

7 I might prove to you, from many other considerations, that religious reasoning is sole master of the passions;

8 but I shall prove it with the greatest force from the fortitude of El'azar, and seven brothers, and their mother, who suffered death in defence of virtue.

9 For all these, contemning pains even unto death, by this contempt, demonstrated that reasoning has command over the passions.

10 For their virtues, then, it is right that I should commend those men who died with their mother at this time in behalf of rectitude; and for their honours, I may count them happy.

---

[97] Here and throughout the word for "reason" is in the Greek λογος logos (Strong's Greek # 3056) which also means "word". It is significant that in the Tanak we are told that the Torah is the "word" (Is. 1:10; 2:3) and that the Greek Septuagint also has λογος for "word" in these passages in Isaiah.

11 For they, winning admiration not only from men in general, but even from the persecutors, for their manliness and endurance, became the means of the destruction of the tyranny against their nation, having conquered the tyrant by their endurance, so that by them their country was purified.

12 But we may now at once enter upon the question, having commenced, as is our wont, with laying down the doctrine, and so proceed to the account of these persons, giving glory to the all wise Elohim.

13 The question, therefore, is, whether reasoning be absolute master of the passions.

14 Let us determine, then, What is reasoning? and what passion? and how many forms of the passions? and whether reasoning bears sway over all of these?

15 Reasoning is, then, intellect accompanied by a life of rectitude, putting foremost the consideration of wisdom.

16 And wisdom is a knowledge of divine and human things, and of their causes.

17 And this is contained in the education of the Torah; by means of which we learn divine things reverently, and human things profitably.

18 And the forms of wisdom are prudence, and justice, and manliness, and temperance.[98]

19 The leading one of these is prudence; by whose means, indeed, it is that reasoning bears rule over the passions.

20 Of the passions, pleasure and pain are the two most comprehensive; and they also by nature refer to the soul.

21 And there are many attendant affections surrounding pleasure and pain.

22 Before pleasure is lust; and after pleasure, joy.

23 And before pain is fear; and after pain is sorrow.

24 Wrath is an affection, common to pleasure and to pain, if any one will pay attention when it comes upon him.

25 And there exists in pleasure a malicious disposition, which is the most multiform of all the affections.

26 In the soul it is arrogance, and love of money, and vaingloriousness, and contention, and faithlessness, and the evil eye[99].

27 In the body it is greediness and gormandizing, and solitary gluttony.

---

[98] Wisdom 8:7

[99] "evil eye" is a Hebrew idiom meaning to be stingy (Prov. 23:6; 28:22)

28 As pleasure and pain are, therefore, two growth of the body and the soul, so there are many offshoots of these passions.

29 And reasoning, the universal husbandman, purging, and pruning these severally, and binding round, and watering, and transplanting, in every way improves the materials of the morals and affections.

30 For reasoning is the leader of the virtues, but it is the sole ruler of the passions. Observe then first, through the very things which stand in the way of temperance, that reasoning is absolute ruler of the passions.

31 Now temperance consists of a command over the lusts.

32 But of the lusts, some belong to the soul, others to the body: and over each of these classes the reasoning appears to bear sway.

33 For whence is it, otherwise, that when urged on to forbidden meats, we reject the gratification which would ensue from them? Is it not because reasoning is able to command the appetites? I believe so.

34 Hence it is, then, that when lusting after water-animals and birds, and fourfooted beasts, and all kinds of food which are forbidden us by the Torah[100], we withhold ourselves through the mastery of reasoning.

35 For the affections of our appetites are resisted by the temperate understanding, and bent back again, and all the impulses of the body are reined in by reasoning.

CHAPTER 2

1 And what wonder? if the lusts of the soul, after participation with what is beautiful, are frustrated,

2 on this ground, therefore, the temperate Yosef is praised in that by reasoning, he subdued, on reflection, the indulgence of sense.[101]

3 For, although young, and ripe for sexual intercourse, he abrogated by reasoning the stimulus of his passions.

4 And it is not merely the stimulus of sensual indulgence, but that of every desire, that reasoning is able to master.

5 For instance, the Torah says, You shall not covet your neighbour's wife, nor anything that belongs to your neighbour.

6 Now, then, since it is the Torah which has forbidden us to desire, I shall much the more easily persuade you, that reasoning is able to govern our lusts, just as it does the affections which are impediments to justice.

---

[100] Lev. 11:1-31; Deur. 14:3-21
[101] Gen. 39:7-12

7 Since in what way is a solitary eater, and a glutton, and a drunkard reclaimed, unless it be clear that reasoning is master of the passions?

8 A man, therefore, who regulates his course by the Torah, even if he be a lover of money, straightway puts force upon his own disposition; lending to the needy without interest[102], and cancelling the debt of the incoming sabbath [year][103].

9 And should a man be parsimonious, he is ruled by the Torah acting through reasoning; so that he does not glean his harvest crops, nor vintage[104]: and in reference to other points we may perceive that it is reasoning that conquers his passions.

10 For the Torah conquers even affection toward parents, not surrendering virtue on their account.

11 And it prevails over marriage love, condemning it when transgressing Torah.

12 And it masters it over the love of parents toward their children, for they punish them for vice; and it domineers over the intimacy of friends, reproving them when wicked.

13 And think it not a strange assertion that reasoning can in behalf of the Torah conquer even enmity.

14 It allows not to cut down the cultivated herbage of an enemy, but preserves it from the destroyers, and collects their fallen ruins[105].

15 And reason appears to be master of the more violent passions, as love of empire and empty boasting, and slander.

16 For the temperate understanding repels all these malignant passions, as it does wrath: for it masters even this.

17 Thus Moshe, when angered against Datan and Aviram, did nothing to them in wrath, but regulated his anger by reasoning[106].

18 For the temperate mind is able, as I said, to be superior to the passions, and to transfer some, and destroy others.

19 For why, else, does our most wise father Ya'akov blame Shim'on and Levi for having irrationally slain the whole race of the Shechemites, saying, Cursed be their anger.[107]

20 For if reasoning did not possess the power of subduing angry affections, he would not have spoken thus.

21 For at the time when Elohim created man, He implanted within him his passions and moral nature.

---

[102] Ex. 22:25
[103] Deut. 15:1-3
[104] Lev. 19:9-10; Deut. 20:19-20
[105] Ex. 23:4-5 (esp. LXX); Deut. 20:19-20
[106] Num. 16:1-35
[107] Gen. 49:7

22 And at that time He enthroned above all the set-apart leader mind, through the medium of the senses.

23 And He gave a Torah to this mind, by living according to which it will maintain a temperate, and just, and good, and manly reign.

24 How, then, a man may say, if reasoning be master of the passions, has it no control over forgetfulness and ignorance?

CHAPTER 3

1 The argument is exceedingly ridiculous: for reasoning does not appear to bear sway over its own affections, but over those of the body,

2 in such a way as that any one of you may not be able to root out desire, but reasoning will enable you to avoid being enslaved to it.

3 One may not be able to root out anger from the soul, but it is possible to withstand anger.

4 Any one of you may not be able to eradicate malice, but reasoning has force to work with you to prevent you yielding to malice.

5 For reasoning is not an eradicator, but an antagonist of the passions.

6 And this may be more clearly comprehended from the thirst of king David[108].

7 For after David had been attacking the Philistines the whole day, he with the soldiers of his nation slew many of them;

8 then when evening came, sweating and very weary, he came to the royal tent, about which the entire host of our ancestors was encamped.

9 Now all the rest of them were at supper;

10 but the king, being very much athirst, although he had numerous springs, could not by their means quench his thirst;

11 but a certain irrational longing for the water in the enemy's camp grew stronger and fiercer upon him, and consumed him with languish.

12 Wherefore his body-guards being troubled at this longing of the king, two valiant young soldiers, reverencing the desire of the king, put on their panoplies, and taking a pitcher, got over the ramparts of the enemies:

13 and unperceived by the guardians of the gate, they went throughout the whole camp of the enemy in quest.

14 And having boldly discovered the fountain, they filled out of it the draught for the king.

---

[108] 2Sam. 23:13-17; 1Chr. 11:15-19

15 But he, though parched with thirst, reasoned that a draught reputed of equal value to blood[109], would be terribly dangerous to his soul.

16 Wherefore, setting up reasoning in opposition to his desire, he poured out the draught to Elohim.

17 For the temperate mind has power to conquer the pressure of the passions, and to quench the fires of excitement,

18 and to wrestle down the pains of the body, however excessive; and, through the excellency of reasoning, to abominate all the assaults of the passions.

19 But the occasion now invites us to give an illustration of temperate reasoning from history.

20 For at a time when our fathers were in possession of undisturbed shalom through obedience to the Torah, and were prosperous, so that Seleucus Nicanor, the king of Asia, both assigned them money for divine service, and accepted their form of government,

21 then certain persons, bringing in new things contrary to the general unanimity, in various ways fell into calamities.

CHAPTER 4

1 For a certain man named Shim'on, who was in opposition to Onias, who once held the Cohen HaGadol-hood for life, and was an honourable and good man, after that by slandering him in every way, he could not injure him with the people, went away as an exile, with the
intention of betraying his country.

2 Whence coming to Apollonius, the military governor of Syria, and Phoenicia, and Cilicia, he said,

3 Having good will to the king's affairs, I am come to inform you that infinite private wealth is laid up in the treasuries of Yerushalayim which do not belong to the Temple, but pertain to king Seleucus.

4 Apollonius, acquainting himself with the particulars of this, praised Shim'on for his care of the king's interests, and going up to Seleucus informed him of the treasure;

5 and getting authority about it, and quickly advancing into our country with the accursed Shim'on and a very heavy force,

6 he said that he came with the commands of the king that he should take the private money of the treasure.

---

[109] 2Sam. 23:17

7 And the nation, indignant at this proclamation, and replying to the effect that it was extremely unfair that those who had committed deposits to the sacred treasury should be deprived of them, resisted as well as they could.

8 But Appolonius went away with threats into the Temple.

9 And the cohenim, with the women and children, having supplicated Elohim to throw his shield over the set-apart, despised place,

10 and Appolonius going up with his armed force to the seizure of the treasure, --there appeared from heaven angels riding on horseback, all radiant in armour, filling them with much fear and trembling.

11 And Apollonius fell half dead upon the court which is open to all nations, and extended his hands to heaven, and implored the Hebrews, with tears, to pray for him, and propitiate the heavenly host.

12 For he said that he had sinned, so as to be consequently worthy of death; and that if he were saved, he would celebrate to all men the blessedness of the set-apart place.

13 Onias the Cohen HaGadol, induced by these words, although for other reasons anxious that king Seleucus should not suppose that Apollonius was slain by human device and not by Divine punishment, prayed for him;

14 and he being thus unexpectedly saved, departed to manifest to the king what had happened to him.

15 But on the death of Seleucus the king, his son Antiochus Epiphanes succeeds to the kingdom: a man of haughty pride and terrible.

16 Who having deposed Onias from the Cohen HaGadolhood, appointed his brother Jason to be Cohen HaGadol:

17 who had made a covenant, if he would give him this authority, to pay yearly three thousand six hundred and sixty talents.

18 And he committed to him the Cohen HaGadolhood and rulership over the nation.

19 And he both changed the manner of living of the people, and perverted their civil customs into all opposition to Torah[110].

20 So that he not only erected a gymnasium on the very citadel of our country, [but neglected] the guardianship of the Temple.

21 At which Divine vengeance being grieved, instigated Antiochus himself against them.

22 For being at war with Ptolemy in Egypt, he heard that on a report of his death being spread abroad, the inhabitants of Yerushalayim had exceedingly rejoiced, and he quickly marched against them.

---

[110] Greek: παρανομειν from the Greek prefix παρα "to oppose" and the Greek word νομος "Torah"

23 And having subdued them, he established a decree that if any of them lived according to the laws of his country he should die.

24 And when he could by no means destroy by his decrees the obedience to the Torah of the nation, but saw all his threats and punishments without effect,

25 for even women, because they continued to circumcise their children, were flung down a precipice along with them, knowing beforehand of the punishment.

26 When, therefore, his decrees were disregarded by the people, he himself compelled by means of tortures every one of this race, by tasting forbidden meats, to abjure the Jewish religion.

CHAPTER 5

1 The tyrant Antiochus, therefore, sitting in public state with his assessors upon a certain lofty place, with his armed troops standing in a circle around him,

2 commanded his spearbearers to seize every one of the Hebrews, and to compel them to taste swine's flesh, and things offered to idols[111].

3 And should any of them be unwilling to eat the accursed food, they were to be tortured on the wheel, and so killed.

4 And when many had been seized, a foremost man of the assembly, a Hebrew, by name El'azar, a cohen by family, learned in the Torah, and advanced in years, and for this reason known to many of the king's followers, was brought near to him.

5 And Antiochus seeing him, said,

6 I would counsel you, old man, before your tortures begin, to taste the swine's flesh, and save your life; for I feel respect for your age and hoary head, which since you have had so long, you appear to me to be no philosopher in retaining the superstition of the Jews.

7 For wherefore, since nature has conferred upon you the most excellent flesh of this animal, do you loathe it?

8 It seems senseless not to enjoy what is pleasant, yet not disgraceful; and from notions of sinfulness, to reject the boons of nature.

9 And you will be acting, I think, still more senselessly, if you follow vain conceits about the
truth.

10 And you will, moreover, be despising me to your own punishment.

---

[111] "things offered to idols" Greek: ελδωλοθυτος which also appears in the Greek New Testament in Acts 15:29; 21:25; 1Cor. 8:1, 4, 7, 10; 10:19 aned Rev. 2:14, 20.

11 Will you not awake from your trifling philosophy? and give up the folly of your notions; and, regaining understanding worthy of your age, search into the truth of an expedient course?

12 and, reverencing my kindly admonition, have pity upon your own years?

13 For, bear in mind, that if there be any power which watches over this religion of yours, it will pardon you for all transgressions of the Torah which you commit through compulsion.

14 While the tyrant incited him in this manner to the unlawful eating of flesh, El'azar begged permission to speak.

15 And having received power to speak, he began thus to deliver himself:

16 We, O Antiochus, who are persuaded that we live under a divine Torah, consider no compulsion to be so forcible as obedience to that Torah;

17 wherefore we consider that we ought not in any point to transgress the Torah.

18 And indeed, were our Torah (as you suppose) not truly divine, and if we wrongly think it divine, we should have no right even in that case to destroy our sense of religion.

19 think not eating the unclean, then, a trifling offense.

20 For transgression of the Torah, whether in small or great matters, is of equal moment;

21 for in either case the Torah is equally slighted.

22 But you deride our philosophy, as though we lived irrationally in it.

23 Yet it instructs us in temperance, so that we are superior to all pleasures and lusts; and it exercises us in manliness, so that we cheerfully undergo every grievance.

24 And it instructs us in justice, so that in all our dealings we render what is due; and it teaches us piety, so that we worship the one only Elohim becomingly.

25 Wherefore it is that we eat not the unclean; for believing that the Torah was established by Elohim, we are convinced that the Creator of the world, in giving his laws, sympathises with our nature.

26 Those things which are convenient to our souls, he has directed us to eat; but those which are repugnant to them, he has interdicted.

27 But, tyrant-like, you not only forcest us to break the Torah, but also to eat, that you may ridicule us as we thus profanely eat:

28 but you shall not have this cause of laughter against me;

29 nor will I transgress the sacred oaths of my forefathers to keep the Torah.

30 No, not if you pluck out my eyes, and consume my entrails.

31 I am not so old, and void of manliness, but that my rational powers are youthful in defence of my religion.

32 Now then; prepare your wheels, and kindle a fiercer flame.

33 I will not so compassionate my old age, as on my account to break the Torah of my country.

34 I will not belie you, O Torah, my instructor! or forsake you, O beloved self-control!

35 I will not put you to shame, O philosopher Reason; or deny you, O honoured priesthood, and knowledge of the Torah.

36 Mouth! you shall not pollute my old age, nor the full stature of a perfect life.

37 My fathers shall receive me pure, not having quailed before your compulsion, though unto death.

38 For over the ungodly you shall tyrannize; but you shall not master it over my thoughts about religion, either by your arguments, or through deeds.

CHAPTER 6

1 When El'azar had in this manner answered the exhortations of the tyrant, the spearbearers came up, and rudely haled El'azar to the instruments of torture.

2 And first, they stripped the old man, adorned as he was with the comeliness of piety.

3 Then tying back his arms and hands, they disdainfully used him with stripes;

4 a herald opposite crying out, Obey the commands of the king.

5 But El'azar, the high-minded and truly noble, as one tortured in a dream, regarded it not all.

6 But raising his eyes on high to heaven, the old man's flesh was stripped off by the scourges, and his blood streamed down, and his sides were pierced through.

7 And falling upon the ground, from his body having no power to support the pains, he yet kept his reasoning upright and unbending.

8 then one of the harsh spearbearers leaped upon his belly as he was falling, to force him upright.

9 But he endured the pains, and despised the cruelty, and persevered through the indignities;

10 and like a noble athlete, the old man, when struck, vanquished his torturers.

11 His countenance sweating, and he panting for breath, he was admired by the very torturers for his courage.

12 Wherefore, partly in pity for his old age,

13 partly from the sympathy of acquaintance, and partly in admiration of his endurance, some of the attendants of the king said,

14 Why do you unreasonably destroy yourself, O El'azar, with these miseries?

15 We will bring you some meat cooked by yourself, and do you save yourself by pretending that you have eaten swine's flesh.

16 And El'azar, as though the advice more painfully tortured him, cried out,

17 Let not us who are children of Avraham be so evil advised as by giving way to make use of an unbecoming pretence;

18 for it were irrational, if having lived up to old age in all truth, and having scrupulously guarded our character for it, we should now turn back,

19 and ourselves should become a pattern of impiety to the young, as being an example of pollution eating.

20 It would be disgraceful if we should live on some short time, and that scorned by all men for cowardice,

21 and be condemned by the tyrant for unmanliness, by not contending to the death for our divine Torah.

22 Wherefore do you, O children of Avraham, die nobly for your religion.

23 You spearbearers of the tyrant, why do you linger?

24 Beholding him so high-minded against misery, and not changing at their pity, they led him to the fire:

25 then with their wickedly-contrived instruments they burnt him on the fire, and poured stinking fluids down into his nostrils.

26 And he being at length burnt down to the bones, and about to expire, raised his eyes Godward, and said,

27 You know, O Elohim, that when I might have been saved, I am slain for the sake of the Torah by tortures of fire.

28 Be merciful to your people, and be satisfied with the punishment of me on their account.

29 Let my blood be a purification for them, and take my life in recompense for theirs.

30 Thus speaking, the set-apart man departed, noble in his torments, and even to the agonies of death resisted in his reasoning for the sake of the Torah.

31 Confessedly, therefore, religious reasoning is master of the passions.

32 For had the passions been superior to reasoning, I would have given them the witness of this mastery.

33 But now, since reasoning conquered the passions, we befittingly awared it the authority of first place.

34 And it is but fair that we should allow, that the power belongs to reasoning, since it masters external miseries.

35 Ridiculous would it be were it not so; and I prove that reasoning has not only mastered pains, but that it is also superior to the pleasures, and withstands them.

CHAPTER 7

1 The reasoning of our father El'azar, like a first-rate pilot, steering the vessel of piety in the sea of passions,

2 and flouted by the threats of the tyrant, and overwhelmed with the breakers of torture,

3 in no way shifted the rudder of piety till it sailed into the harbour of victory over death.

4 Not so has ever a city, when besieged, held out against many and various machines, as did that set-apart man, when his pious soul was tried with the fiery trial of tortures and rackings, move his besiegers through the religious reasoning that shielded him.

5 For father El'azar, projecting his disposition, broke the raging waves of the passions as with a jutting promontory.

6 O cohen worthy of the priesthood! you did not pollute your sacred teeth; nor make your appetite, which had always embraced the clean and lawful, a partaker of profanity.

7 O harmonizer with the Torah, and sage devoted to a divine life!

8 Of such a character ought those to be who perform the duties of the Torah at the risk of their own blood, and defend it with generous sweat by sufferings even unto death.

9 You, father, have gloriously established our right government by your endurance; and making of much account our service past, prevented its destruction, and, by your deeds, have made credible the words of philosophy.

10 O aged man of more power than tortures, elder more vigorous than fire, greatest king over the passions, El'azar!

11 For as father Aharon, armed with a censer, hastening through the consuming fire, vanquished the flame-bearing angel,[112]

_____
[112] Num. 16:46-50

12 so, El'azar, the descendant of Aharon, wasted away by the fire, did not give up his reasoning.

13 And, what is most wonderful, though an old man, though the labours of his body were now spent, and his fibres were relaxed, and his sinews worn out, he recovered youth.

14 By the spirit of reasoning, and the reasoning of Yitzach, he rendered powerless the many-headed instrument.

15 O blessed old age, and reverend hoar head, and life obedient to the Torah, which the faithful seal of death perfected.

16 If, then, an old man, through religion, despised tortures even unto death, confessedly religious reasoning is ruler of the passions.

17 But perhaps some might say, It is not all who conquer passions, as all do not possess wise reasoning.

18 But they who have meditated upon religion with their whole heart, these alone can master the passions of the flesh;

19 they who believe that to Elohim they die not; for, as our forefathers, Avraham, Yitzach, Ya'akov, they live to Elohim[113].

20 This circumstance, then, is by no means an objection, that some who have weak reasoning, are governed by their passions:

21 since what person, walking religiously by the whole rule of philosophy, and believing in Elohim,

22 and knowing that it is a blessed thing to endure all kinds of hardships for virtue, would not, for the sake of religion, master his passion?

23 For the wise and brave man only is master over his passions.

24 Whence it is, that even boys, imbued with the philosophy of religious reasoning, have conquered still more bitter tortures:

25 for when the tyrant was manifestly vanquished in his first attempt, in being unable to force the old man to eat the unclean thing,-

CHAPTER 8

1 Then, indeed, vehemently swayed with passion, he commanded to bring others of the adult Hebrews, and if they would eat of the unclean thing, to let them go when they had eaten; but if they objected, to torment them more grievously.

2 The tyrant having given this charge, seven brothers were brought into his presence, along with their aged mother, handsome, and modest, and well-born, and altogether comely.

---

[113] Mk. 12:26

3 Whom, when the tyrant beheld, encircling their mother as in a dance, he was pleased at them; and being struck with their becoming and ingenuous mien, smiled upon them, and calling them near, said:

4 O youths, with favourable feelings, I admire the beauty of each of you; and greatly honouring so numerous a band of brothers, I not only counsel you not to share the madness of the old man who has been tortured before,

5 but I do beg you to yield, and to enjoy my friendship; for I possess the power, not only of punishing those who disobey my commands, but of doing good to those who obey them.

6 Put confidence in me, then, and you shall receive places of authority in my government, if you forsake your national ordinance,

7 and, conforming to the Greek way of life, alter your rule, and revel in youth's delights.

8 For if you provoke me by your disobedience, you will compel me to destroy you, every one, with terrible punishments by tortures.

9 Have mercy, then, upon your own selves, whom I, although an enemy, compassionate for your age and comeliness.

10 Will you not reason upon this--that if you disobey, there will be nothing left for you but to die in tortures?

11 Thus speaking, he ordered the instruments of torture to be brought forward, that very fear might prevail upon them to eat unclean meat.

12 And when the spearman brought forward the wheels, and the racks, and the hooks, and catapeltae, and caldrons, pans, and finger-racks, and iron claws and wedges, and bellows, the tyrant continue:

13 Fear, young men, and the righteousness which you worship will be merciful to you if you err from compulsion.

14 Now they having listened to these words of persuasion, and seeing the fearful instruments, not only were not afraid, but even answered the arguments of the tyrant, and through their good reasoning destroyed his power.

15 Now let us consider the matter: had any of them been weak-spirited and cowardly among them, what reasonings would they have employed but these?

16 O wretched that we are, and exceeding senseless! when the king exhorts us, and calls us to his bounty, should we not obey him?

17 Why do we cheer ourselves with vain counsels, and venture upon a disobedience bringing death?

18 Shall we not fear, O brothers, the instruments of torture and weigh the threatenings of torment and shun this vain-glory and destructive pride?

19 Let us have compassion upon our age and relent over the years of our mother.

20 And let us bear in mind that we shall be dying as rebels.

21 And Divine Justice will pardon us if we fear the king through necessity.

22 Why withdraw ourselves from a most sweet life, and deprive ourselves of this pleasant world?

23 Let us not oppose necessity, nor seek vain-glory by our own excruciation.

24 The Torah itself is not forward to put us to death, if we dread torture.

25 Whence has such angry zeal taken root in us, and such fatal obstinacy approved itself to us, when we might live unmolested by the king?

26 But nothing of this kind did the young men say or think when about to be tortured.

27 For they were well aware of the sufferings, and masters of the pains. So that as soon as the tyrant had ceased counselling them to eat the unclean, they altogether with one voice, as from the same heart said:

CHAPTER 9

1 Why delay you, O tyrant? for we are readier to die than to transgress the injunctions of our fathers.

2 And we should be disgracing our fathers if we did not obey the Torah, and take knowledge for our guide.

3 O tyrant, counsellor of Torah-breaking, do not, hating us as you do, pity us more than we pity ourselves.

4 For we account escape to be worse than death.

5 And you think to scare us, by threatening us with death by tortures, as though you had learned nothing by the death of El'azar.

6 But if aged men of the Hebrews have died in the cause of religion after enduring torture, more rightly should we younger men die, scorning your cruel tortures, which our aged instructor overcame.

7 Make the attempt, then, O tyrant; and if you put us to death for our religion, think not that you harm us by torturing us.

8 For we through this ill-treatment and endurance shall bear off the rewards of virtue.

9 But you, for the wicked and despotic slaughter of us, shall, from the Divine vengeance, endure eternal torture by fire.

10 When they had thus spoken, the tyrant was not only exasperated against them as being refractory, but enraged with them as being ungrateful.

11 So that, at his bidding, the torturers brought forth the oldest of them, and tearing through his tunic, bound his hands and arms on each side with thongs.

12 And when they had laboured hard without effect in scourging him, they hurled him upon the wheel.

13 And the noble youth, extended upon this, became dislocated.

14 And with every member disjointed, he exclaimed in expostulation,

15 O most accursed tyrant, and enemy of heavenly justice, and cruel-hearted, I am no murderer, nor sacrilegious man, whom you thus ill-use; but a defender of the Divine Torah.

16 And when the spearmen said, Consent to eat, that you may be released from your tortures,--

17 he answered, Not so powerful, O accursed ministers, is your wheel, as to stifle my reasoning; cut my limbs, and burn my flesh, and twist my joints.

18 For through all my torments I will convince you that the children of the Hebrews are alone unconquered in behalf of virtue.

19 While he was saying this, they heaped up fuel, and setting fire to it, strained him upon the wheel still more.

20 And the wheel was defiled all over with blood, and the hot ashes were quenched by the droppings of gore, and pieces of flesh were scattered about the axles of the machine.

21 And although the framework of his bones was now destroyed the high-minded and Avrahamic youth did not groan.

22 But, as though transformed by fire into immortality, he nobly endured the rackings, saying

23 Imitate me, O brothers, nor ever desert your station, nor abjure my brotherhood in courage: fight the set-apart and honourable fight of religion;

24 by which means our just and paternal Providence, becoming merciful to the nation, will punish the pestilent tyrant.

25 And saying this, the revered youth abruptly closed his life.

26 And when all admired his courageous soul, the spearmen brought forward him who was second in point of age, and having put on iron claws, bound him with pointed hooks to the catapelt.

27 And when, on enquiring whether he would eat before he was tortured, they heard his noble sentiment,

28 after they with the iron claws had violently dragged all the flesh from the neck to the chin, the panther- like beasts tore off the very skin of his head: but he, bearing with firmness this misery, said,

29 How sweet is every form of death for the religion of our fathers! and he said to the tyrant,

30 Think you not, most cruel of all tyrants, that you are now tortured more than I, finding your overweening conception of tyranny conquered by our patience in behalf of our religion?

31 For I lighten my suffering by the pleasures which are connected with virtue.

32 But you are tortured with threatenings for impiety; and you shall not escape, most corrupt tyrant, the vengeance of Divine wrath.

CHAPTER 10

1 Now this one, having endured this praiseworthy death, the third was brought along, and exhorted by many to taste and save his life.

2 But he cried out and said, Know you not, that the father of those who are dead, begat me also; and that the same mother bare me; and that I was brought up in the same tenets?

3 I abjure not the noble relationship of my brothers.

4 Now then, whatever instrument of vengeance you have, apply it to my body, for you are not able to touch, even if you wish it, my soul.

5 But they, highly incensed at his boldness of speech, dislocated his hands and feet with racking engines, and wrenching them from their sockets, dismembered him.

6 And they dragged round his fingers, and his arms, and his legs, and his ankles.

7 And not being able by any means to strangle him, they tore off his skin, together with the extreme tips of his fingers, flayed him, and then haled him to the wheel;

8 around which his vertebral joints were loosened, and he saw his own flesh torn to shreds, and streams of blood flowing from his entrails.

9 And when about to die, he said,

10 We, O accursed tyrant, suffer this for the sake of Divine education and virtue.

11 But you, for your impiety and blood-shedding, shall endure indissoluble torments.

12 And thus having died worthily of his brothers, they dragged forward the fourth, saying,

13 Do not you share the madness of your brothers: but give regard to the king, and save yourself.

14 But he said to them, You have not a fire so scorching as to make me play the coward.

15 By the blessed death of my brothers, and the eternal punishment of the tyrant, and the glorious life of the pious, I will not repudiate the noble brotherhood.

16 Invent, O tyrant, tortures; that you may learn, even through them, that I am the brother of those tormented before.

17 When he had said this, the blood-thirsty, and murderous, and unhallowed Antiochus ordered his tongue to be cut out.

18 But he said, Even if you take away the organ of speech, yet Elohim hears the silent.

19 Behold, my tongue is extended, cut it off; for not for that halt you extirpate our reasoning.

20 Gladly do we lose our limbs in behalf of Elohim.

21 But Elohim shall speedly find you, since you cut off the tongue, the instrument of divine melody.

CHAPTER 11

1 And when he had died, disfigured in his torments, the fifth leaped forward, and said,

2 I intend not, O tyrant, to get excused from the torment which is in behalf of virtue.

3 But I have come of my own accord, that by the death of me, you may owe heavenly vengeance a punishment for more crimes.

4 O you hater of virtue and of men, what have we done that you thus revel in our blood?

5 Does it seem evil to you that we worship the Founder of all things, and live according to his surpassing Torah?

6 But this is worthy of honours, not torments;

7 had you been capable of the higher feelings of men, and possessed the hope of salvation from Elohim.

8 Behold now, being alien from Elohim, you make war against those who are religious toward Elohim.

9 As he said this, the spearbearers bound him, and drew him to the catapelt:

10 to which binding him at his knees, and fastening them with iron fetters, they bent down his loins upon the wedge of the wheel; and his body was then dismembered, scorpion-fashion.

11 With his breath thus confined, and his body strangled, he said,

12 A great favour you bestow upon us, O tyrant, by enabling us to manifest our adherence to the Torah by means of nobler sufferings.

13 He also being dead, the sixth, quite a youth, was brought out; and on the tyrant asking him whether he would eat and be delivered, he said,

14 I am indeed younger than my brothers, but in understanding I am as old;

15 for having been born and reared unto the same end, we are bound to die also in behalf of the same cause.

16 So that if you think proper to torment us for not eating the unclean;--torment!

17 As he said this, they brought him to the wheel.

18 Extended upon which, with limbs racked and dislocated, he was gradually roasted from beneath.

19 And having heated sharp spits, they approached them to his back; and having transfixed his sides, they burned away his entrails.

20 And he, while tormented, said, O period good and set-apart, in which, for the sake of religion, we brothers have been called to the contest of pain, and have not been conquered.

21 For religious understanding, O tyrant, is unconquered.

22 Armed with upright virtue, I also shall depart with my brothers.

23 I, too, bearing with me a great avenger, O deviser of tortures, and enemy of the truly pious.

24 We six youths have destroyed your tyranny.

25 For is not your inability to overrule our reasoning, and to compel us to eat the unclean, your destruction?

26 Your fire is cold to us, your catapelts are painless, and your violence harmless.

27 For the guards not of a tyrant but of a divine Torah are our defenders: through this we keep our reasoning unconquered.

CHAPTER 12

1 When he, too, had undergone blessed martyrdom, and died in the caldron into which he had been thrown, the seventh, the youngest of all, came forward:

2 whom the tyrant pitying, though he had been dreadfully reproached by his brothers,

3 seeing him already encompassed with chains, had him brought nearer, and endeavoured to counsel him, saying,

4 You see the end of the madness of your brothers: for they have died in torture through disobedience; and you, if disobedient, having been miserably tormented, will yourself perish prematurely.

5 But if you obey, you shall be my friend, and have a charge over the affairs of the kingdom.

6 And having thus exhorted him, he sent for the mother of the boy; that, by condoling with her for the loss of so many sons, he might incline her, through the hope of safety, to render the survivor obedient.

7 And he, after his mother had urged him on in the Hebrew tongue, (as we shall soon relate) says,

8 Release me that I may speak to the king and all his friends.

9 And they, rejoicing exceedingly at the promise of the youth, quickly let him go.

10 And he, running up to the pans, said,

11 Impious tyrant, and most blasphemous man, were you not ashamed, having received prosperity and a kingdom from Elohim, to slay His servants, and to rack the doers of godliness?

12 Wherefore the divine vengeance is reserving you for eternal fire and torments, which shall cling to you for all time.

13 Were you not ashamed, man as you are, yet most savage, to cut out the tongues of men of like feeling and origin, and having thus abused to torture them?

14 But they, bravely dying, fulfilled their religion towards Elohim.

15 But you shall groan according to your deserts for having slain without cause the champions of virtue.

16 Wherefore, he continued, I myself, being about to die,

17 will not forsake my brothers.

18 And I call upon the Elohim of my fathers to be merciful to my race.

19 But you, both living and dead, he will punish.

20 Thus having prayed, he hurled himself into the pans; and so expired.

CHAPTER 13

1 If then, the seven brothers despised troubles even unto death, it is confessed on all sides that righteous reasoning is absolute master over the passions.

2 For just as if, had they as slaves to the passions, eaten of the unholy, we should have said that they had been conquered by the;

3 now it is not so: but by means of the reasoning which is praised by Elohim, they mastered their passions.

4 And it is impossible to overlook the leadership of reflection: for it gained the victory over both passions and troubles.

5 How, then, can we avoid according to these men mastery of passion through right reasoning, since they drew not back from the pains of fire?

6 For just as by means of towers projecting in front of harbours men break the threatening waves, and thus assure a still course to vessels entering port,

7 so that seven-towered right- reasoning of the young men, securing the harbour of religion, conquered the intemperance of passions.

8 For having arranged a set-apart choir of piety, they encouraged one another, saying,

9 Brothers, may we die brotherly for the Torah. Let us imitate the three young men in Assyria who despised the equally afflicting furnace.

10 Let us not be cowards in the manifestation of piety.

11 And one said, Courage, brother; and another, Nobly endure.

12 And another, Remember of what stock you are; and by the hand of our father Yitzach endured to be slain for the sake of piety.

13 And one and all, looking on each other serene and confident, said, Let us sacrifice with all our heart our souls to Elohim who gave them, and employ our bodies for the keeping of the Torah.

14 Let us not fear him who thinks he kills;

15 for great is the trial of soul and danger of eternal torment laid up for those who transgress the commandment of Elohim.

16 Let us arm ourselves, therefore, in the abnegation of the divine reasoning.

17 If we suffer thus, Avraham, and Yitzach, and Ya'akov will receive us, and all the fathers will commend us.

18 And as each one of the brothers was haled away, the rest exclaimed, Disgrace us not, O brother, nor falsify those who died before you.

19 Now you are not ignorant of the charm of brotherhood, which the Divine and all wise Providence has imparted through fathers to children, and has engendered through the mother's womb.

20 In which these brothers having remained an equal time, and having been formed for the same period, and been increased by the same blood, and having been perfected through the same principle of life,

21 and having been brought forth at equal intervals, and having sucked milk from the same fountains, hence their brotherly souls are reared up lovingly together;

22 and increase the more powerfully by reason of this simultaneous rearing, and by daily intercourse, and by other education, and exercise in the Torah of Elohim.

23 Brotherly love being thus sympathetically constituted, the seven brothers had a more sympathetic mutual harmony.

24 For being educated in the same Torah, and practising the same virtues, and reared up in a just course of life, they increased this harmony with each other.

25 For a like ardour for what is right and honourable increased their fellow-feeling towards each other.

26 For it acting along with religion, made their brotherly feeling more desirable to them.

27 And yet, although nature and intercourse and virtuous morals increased their brotherly love those who were left endured to behold their brothers, who were ill-used for their religion, tortured even unto death.

CHAPTER 14

1 And more that this, they even urged them on to this ill-treatment; so that they not only despised pains themselves, but they even got the better of their affections of brotherly love.

2 O reasonings more royal than a king, and freer than freemen!

3 Sacred and harmonious concert of the seven brothers as concerning piety!

4 None of the seven youths turned cowardly, or shrank back from death.

5 But all of them, as though running the road to immortality, hastened on to death through tortures.

6 For just as hands and feet are moved sympathetically with the directions of the soul, so those set-apart youths agreed unto death for religion's sake, as through the immortal soul of religion.

7 O set-apart seven of harmonious brothers! for as the seven days of creation, about religion,

8 so the youths, circling around the number seven, annulled the fear of torments.

9 We now shudder at the recital of the affliction of those young men; but they not only beheld, and not only heard the immediate execution of the threat, but undergoing it, persevered; and that through the pains of fire.

10 And what could be more painful? for the power of fire, being sharp and quick, speedily dissolved their bodies.

11 And think it not wonderful that reasoning bore rule over those men in their torments, when even a woman's mind despised more manifold pains.

12 For the mother of those seven youths endured the rackings of each of her children.

13 And consider how comprehensive is the love of offspring, which draws every one to sympathy of affection,

14 where irrational animals possess a similar sympathy and love for their offspring with men.

15 The tame birds frequenting the roofs of our houses, defend their fledglings.

16 Others build their nests, and hatch their young, in the tops of mountains and in the precipices of valleys, and the holes and tops of trees, and keep off the intruder.

17 And if not able to do this, they fly circling round them in agony of affection, calling out in their own note, and save their offspring in whatever manner they are able.

18 But why should we point attention to the sympathy toward children shewn by irrational animals?

19 The very bees, at the season of honey-making, attack all who approach; and pierce with their sting, as with a sword, those who draw near their hive, and repel them even unto death.

20 But sympathy with her children did not turn aside the mother of the young men, who had a spirit kindred with that of Avraham.

CHAPTER 15

1 O reasoning of the sons, master over the passions, and religion more desirable to a mother than progeny!

2 The mother, when two things were set before here, religion and the safety of her seven sons for a time, on the conditional promise of a tyrant,

3 rather elected the religion which according to Elohim preserves to eternal life.

4 O in what way can I describe ethically the affections of parents toward their children, the resemblance of soul and of form engrafted into the small type of a child in a wonderful manner, especially through the greater sympathy of mothers with the feelings of those born of them!

5 for by how much mothers are by nature weak in disposition and prolific in offspring, by so much the fonder they are of children.

6 And of all mothers the mother of the seven was the fondest of children, who in seven childbirths had deeply engendered love toward them;

7 and through her many pains undergone in connection with each one, was compelled to feel sympathy with them;

8 yet, through fear of Elohim, she neglected the temporary salvation of her children.

9 Not but that, on account of the excellent disposition to the Torah, her maternal affection toward them was increased.

10 For they were both just and temperate, and manly, and high-minded, and fond of their brothers, and so fond of their mother that even unto death they obeyed her by observing the Torah.

11 And yet, though there were so many circumstances connected with love of children to draw on a mother to sympathy, in the case of none of them were the various tortures able to pervert her principle.

12 But she inclined each one separately and all together to death for religion.

13 O set-apart nature and parental feeling, and reward of bringing up children, and unconquerable maternal affection!

14 At the racking and roasting of each one of them, the observant mother was prevented by religion from changing.

15 She beheld her children's flesh dissolving around the fire; and their extremities quivering on the ground, and the flesh of their heads dropped forwards down to their beards, like masks.

16 O you mother, who wast tried at this time with bitterer pangs than those of parturition!

17 O you only woman who have brought forth perfect holiness!

18 Thy first-born, expiring, turned you not; nor the second, looking miserable in his torments; nor the third, breathing out his soul.

19 Nor when you did behold the eyes of each of them looking sternly upon their tortures, and their nostrils foreboding death, did you weep!

20 When you did see children's flesh heaped upon children's flesh that had been torn off, heads decapitated upon heads, dead falling upon the dead, and a choir of children turned through torture into a burying ground, you lamented not.

21 Not so do siren melodies, or songs of swans, attract the hearers to listening, O voices of children calling upon your mother in the midst of torments!

22 With what and what manner of torments was the mother herself tortured, as her sons were undergoing the wheel and the fires!

23 But religious reasoning, having strengthened her courage in the midst of suferings, enabled her to forego, for the time, parental love.
24 Although beholding the destruction of seven children, the noble mother, after one embrace, stripped off [her feelings] through faith in Elohim.
25 For just as in a council-room, beholding in her own soul vehement counsellors, nature and parentage and love of her children, and the racking of her children,
26 she holding two votes, one for the death, the other for the preservation of her children,
27 did not lean to that which would have saved her children for the safety of a brief space.
28 But this daughter of Avraham remembered his set-apart fortitude.
29 O set-apart mother of a nation avenger of the Torah, and defender of religion, and prime bearer in the battle of the affections!
30 O you nobler in endurance than males, and more manly than men in patience!
31 For as the ark of Noach, bearing the world in the world-filling flood, bore up against the waves,[114]
32 so you, the guardian of the Torah, when surrounded on every side by the flood of passions, and straitened by violent storms which were the torments of they children, did bear up nobly against the storms against religion.

CHAPTER 16

1 If, then, even a woman, and that an aged one, and the mother of seven children, endured to see her children's torments even unto death, confessedly religious reasoning is master even of the passions.
2 I have proved, then, that not only men have obtained the mastery of their passions, but also that a woman despised the greatest torments.
3 And not so fierce were the lions round Daniel[115], nor the furnace of Misha'el[116] burning with most vehement fires as that natural love of children burned within her, when she beheld her seven sons tortured.
4 But with the reasoning of religion the mother quenched passions so great and powerful.

---

[114] Gen. 7
[115] Dan. 6:1-24
[116] Dan. 1:7; 3:19-30

5 For we must consider also this: that, had the woman been faint hearted, as being their other, she would have lamented over them; and perhaps might have spoken thus:

6 Ah! wretched I, and many times miserable; who having born seven sons, have become the mother of none.

7 O seven useless childbirths, and seven profitless periods of labour, and fruitless givings of suck, and miserable nursings at the breast.

8 Vainly, for your sakes, O sons, have I endured many pangs, and the more difficult anxieties of rearing.

9 Alas, of my children, some of you unmarried, and some who have married to no profit, I shall not see your children, nor be felicitated as a grandmother.

10 Ah, that I who had many and fair children, should be a lone widow full of sorrows!

11 Nor, should I die, shall I have a son to bury me. But with such a lament as this the set-apart and Elohim-fearing mother bewailed none of them.

12 Nor did she divert any of them from death, nor grieve for them as for the dead.

13 But as one possessed with an adamantine mind, and as one bringing forth again her full number of sons to immortality, she rather with supplication exhorted them to death in behalf of religion.

14 O woman, soldier of Elohim for religion, you, aged and a female, have conquered through endurance even a tyrant; and though but weak, have been found more powerful in deeds and words.

15 For when you wast seized along with your children, you stood looking upon El'azar in torments, and said to your sons in the Hebrew tongue,

16 O sons, noble is the contest; to which you being called as a witness for the nation, strive zealously for the laws of your country.

17 For it were disgraceful that this old man should endure pains for the sake of righteousness, and that you who are younger should be afraid of the tortures.

18 Remember that through Elohim you obtained existence, and have enjoyed it.

19 And on this second account you ought to bear every affliction because of Elohim.

20 For whom also our father Avraham was forward to sacrifice Yitzach our progenitor, and shuddered not at the sight of his own paternal hand descending down with the sword upon him.

21 And the righteous Daniel was cast unto the lions; and Hananyah, and 'Azaryah, and Misha'el, were slung out into a furnace of fire; yet they endured through Elohim.[117]

22 You, then, having the same faith towards Elohim, be not troubled.

23 For it is unreasonable that they who know religion should not stand up against troubles.

24 With these arguments, the mother of seven, exhorting each of her sons, overpersuaded them from transgressing the commandment of Elohim.

25 And they saw this, too, that they who die for Elohim, live to Elohim; as Avraham, and Yitzach, and Ya'akov, and all the patriarchs.

CHAPTER 17

1 And some of the spearbearers said, that when she herself was about to be seized for the purpose of being put to death, she threw herself upon the pile, rather than they should touch her person.

2 O you mother, who together with seven children did destroy the violence of the tyrant, and render void his wicked intentions, and exhibit the nobleness of faith!

3 For you, as an house bravely built upon the pillar of your children, did bear without swaying, the shock of tortures.

4 Be of good cheer, therefore, O set-apart-minded mother! holding the firm [substance of the] hope of your steadfastness with Elohim.

5 Not so gracious does the moon appear with the stars in heaven, as you are established honourable before Elohim, and fixed in the firmament with your sons who you did illuminate with religion to the stars.

6 For your bearing of children was after the fashion of a child of Avraham.

7 And, were it lawful for us to paint as on a tablet the religion of your story, the spectators would not shudder at beholding the mother of seven children enduring for the sake of religion various tortures even unto death.

8 And it had been a worth while thing to have inscribed upon the tomb itself these words as a memorial to those of the nation,

9 Here an aged cohen, and an aged woman, and seven sons, are buried through the violence of a tyrant, who wished to destroy the polity of the Hebrews.

---

[117] Dan. 3

10 These also avenged their nation, looking unto Elohim, and enduring torments unto death.

11 For it was truly a divine contest which was carried through by them.

12 For at that time virtue presided over the contest, approving the victory through endurance, namely, immortality, eternal life.

13 El'azar was the first to contend: and the mother of the seven children entered the contest; and the brothers contended.

14 The tyrant was the opposite; and the world and living men were the spectators.

15 And reverence for Elohim conquered, and crowned her own athletes.

16 Who did not admire those champions of true legislation? who were not astonied?

17 The tyrant himself, and all their council, admired their endurance;

18 through which, also, they now stand beside the divine throne, and live a blessed life.

19 For Moshe says, And all the set-apart-ones are under your hands[118].

20 These, therefore, having been sanctified through Elohim, have been honoured not only with this honour, but that also by their means the enemy did not overcome our nation;

21 and that the tyrant was punished, and their country purified.

22 For they became the ransom to the sin of the nation; and the Divine Providence saved Yisrael, aforetime afflicted, by the blood of those pious ones, and the propitiatory death.

23 For the tyrant Antiochus, looking to their manly virtue, and to their endurance in torture, proclaimed that endurance as an example to his soldiers.

24 And they proved to be to him noble and brave for land battles and for sieges; and he conquered and stormed the towns of all his enemies.

CHAPTER 18

1 O Israelites children, descendants of the seed of Avraham, obey this Torah, and in every way be religious.

2 Knowing that religious reasoning is master of the passions, and those not only inward but outward.

3 When those persons giving up their bodies to pains for the sake of religion, were not only admired by men, but were deemed worthy of a divine portion.

---

[118] Dt 33:3

4 And the nation through them obtained shalom, and having renewed the observance of the Torah in their country, drove the enemy out of the land.

5 And the tyrant Antiochus was both punished upon earth, and is punished now he is dead; for when he was quite unable to compel the Israelites to adopt foreign customs, and to desert the manner of life of their fathers,

6 then, departing from Yerushalayim, he made war against the Persians.

7 And the righteous mother of the seven children space also as follows to her offspring: I was a pure virgin, and went not beyond my father's house; but I took care of the built-up rib[119].

8 No destroyer of the desert, [or] ravisher of the plain[120], injured me; nor did the destructive, deceitful snake, make spoil of my chaste virginity; and I remained with my husband during the period of my prime.

9 And these my children, having arrived at maturity, their father died: blessed was he! for having sought out a life of fertility in children, he was not grieved with a period of loss of children.

10 And he used to teach you, when yet with you, the Torah and the Prophets.

11 He used to read to you the slaying of Hevel by Kayin[121], and the offering up of Yitzach[122], and the imprisonment of Yosef[123].

12 And he used to tell you of the zealous Pinchas[124]; and informed you of Hananyah and 'Azaryah, and Misha'el in the fire.

13 And he used to glorify Daniel, who was in the den of lions[125], and pronounce him blessed.

14 And he used to put you in mind of the Scripture of Yesha'yahu, which says, Even if you pass through the fire, it shall not burn you[126].

15 He chanted to you David, the Psalmist, who says, Many are the afflictions of the just[127].

16 He declared the proverbs of Shlomo, who says, He is a tree of life to all those who do His will[128].

---

[119] Gen. 2:22
[120] Deut. 22:25-27
[121] Gen. 4:2-15
[122] Gen. 22:1-19
[123] Gen. 39:1-23
[124] Num. 25:1-9
[125] Dan. 6:1-24
[126] Is 43:2
[127] Ps 34:19

17 He used to verify Yechezk'el, who said, Shall these dry bones live?[129]

18 For he did not forget the song which Moshe taught, proclaiming, I will kill, and I will make to live.[130]

19 This is our life, and the length of our days[131].

20 O that bitter, and yet not bitter, day when the bitter tyrant of the Greeks, quenching fire with fire in his cruel caldrons, brought with boiling rage the seven sons of the daughter of Avraham to the catapelt, and to all his torments!

21 He pierced the balls of their eyes, and cut out their tongues, and put them to death with varied tortures.

22 Wherefore divine retribution pursued and will pursue the pestilent wretch.

23 But the children of Avraham, with their victorious mother, are assembled together to the choir of their father; having received pure and immortal souls from Elohim.

24 To whom be glory for ever and ever. Amen.

---

[128] Prov. 3:18
[129] Ezek 37:2-3
[130] Deut. 32:29
[131] Deut. 30:20; 32:39

Appendix
Harmonic Chronology of 1, 2 & 4 Maccabees

Event	1Maccabees	2Maccabees	4Maccabees
The Rise of the Seleucid Empire	1:1-10		
An attempt to take the Temple treasury		3:1-40	3:19-4:14
The plot against Onias		4:1-6	
Jason becomes Cohen HaGadol	1:11-15	4:7-22	
Menelaus becomes Cohen HaGadol		4:23-50	
Antiochus Epiphanes comes to Jerusalem	1:16-40	5:1-27	4:15-26
The Abomination of Desolation	1:41-64	6:1-6	
Martyrs		6:7-17	
Eleazer is martyred		6:18-31	5-7
Martyrdom of Hannah and her seven sons		7	8-18
The revolt begins	2:1-48	8:1-7	
Mattithias dies	2:49-70		
Various battles	3:1-4:35	8:8-36	

Antiochus' illness		9:1-12	
Antiochus dies	(6:1-17)	9:13-29	
Cleansing of the Temple	4:36-61	10:1-9	
More battles	5:1-68		
Antiochus dies	6:1-17	(9:13-29)	
Various battles	6:18-63	10:10-13:26	
Demetrius becomes king	7:1-4	14:1-10	
Appointments of Nicanor and Alcimus	7:5-25	14:11-14	
Nicanor and Judas	7:26-38	14:15-46	
Death of Nicanor	7:39-50	15:1-36	

Celebration of Channukah

The central element of Channukh celebration is the lighting of the Channukiah, a special Channukah menorah. Unlike the seven branched menorah, the Chanukah menorah has nine branches. Eight of these are for each of the eight days of Channukah and one, called the Shamash (helper) is used to light the other eight. This ninth light is usually elevated from the other eight so as to distinguish it from the others.

One each of the eight nights of Channukah an additional candle (or lamp) is lit so that on the eighth day, all eight are burning. The first night the light on the far right is lit. On the second night the two on the farthest right are lit and so on. Also each night we begin by lighting the new light first and then working our way back to the beginning (to the left) so that the first comes last and the last comes first.

On Friday evenings the Channukah candle (or oil) is lit early, before sun down and before the Sabbath candles. On Saturday night the Channukah candle is lit after havdalah (the close of Sabbath).

Each night immediately after lighting the Channukah lights, the following prayer is said:

ברוך אתה יהוה אלהינו מלך העולם
אשר קדשנו במצותיו וצונו להדליק נר של חנכה
ברוך אתה יהוה אלהינו מלך העולם
שעשה נסים לאבותינו בימים ההם בזמן הזה

Baruch ata YHWH Eloheynu Melech Ha-Olam
Asher kidshanu b'mitzvotav vitzivanu l'hadlik ner shel Channukah
Baruch ata YHWH Eloheynu Melech Ha-Olam
She-asa nisim la'avoteynu bayamim haheym ba-zman hazeh.

Blessed are You YHWH our Elohim, King of the universe
Who has sanctified us by your commandments and commanded us to kindle the light of Channukah.
Blessed are You YHWH our Elohim, King of the universe
Who worked miracles for our fathers in days of old, at this season.

On the first night of Channukah we also recite the Shehecheyanu, the traditional prayer marking special occasions:

$$\text{ברוך אתה יהוה אלהינו מלך העולם}$$
$$\text{שהחינו וקימנו והגיענו לזמן הזה}$$

Baruch ata YHWH Eloheynu Melech Ha-Olam
Shehecheyanu v'kiy'manu v'higanu la-zman hazeh.

Blessed are You YHWH our Elohim, King of the universe
Who has kept us in life, and has preserved us, and enabled us to reach this season.

Since Channukah is eight days long, we suggest studying each of the four books of Maccabees for two days, thus progressing up the four levels of understanding as follows:

Days 1-2	1Maccabees	Pashat
Days 3-4	2Maccabees	Remez
Days 5-6	3Maccabees	Drash
Days 7-8	4Maccabees	Sod

Channukah is also often celebrated by eating foods cooked in oil. Traditional favorites are potato latkes, a sort of potato pancake. Another favorite are homemade donuts fried in oil.

Many families also exchange gifts at Channukah. Some see this as a custom borrowed from Christmas, however some evidence indicates that gift-exchanging was a common part of Jewish festival celebration in general, and may have been incorporated into Christmas from Channukah. It appears that anciently Jewish festival celebration often included gift-giving. The Scriptures mention this custom in connection with Rosh Hashanna (Neh. 8:10) and Purim (Ester 9:22) and it may well have been practiced in connection with Channukah as well.

Another popular Channukah custom is the dreidl game. A dreidl is a four sided top, with a Hebrew letter on each of the four sides. The game is played by spinning the top, when the top finally comes to rest, one of the four letters is facing up (similar to rolling dice). The letters on the dreidl are:

נ Nun

ג Gimel

ה Hey

ש Shin

These four letters stand for the phrase:

נס גדול היה שם

Nes Gadol Haya Sham

"A great miracle happened there."

Depending on which letter comes up the player does one of four things:

ג Take everything from the pot.

ה Take half of the pot.

ש Put one in the pot.

נ Do nothing.

Children often play the dreidl game with candy coins called "gelt". There is a tradition the game was used to conceal Torah study in times when Torah study was outlawed. Men would be gathered around studying Torah and if they were discovered by the authorities they would pretend to be gathered around gambling.